DATE		
MAY 11 '79		
MAY 24 '79		
FEB 20 '81		
NOV 08 1988		
FEB 1 2 1990		
OCT 2 9 1990		
JAN C 7 '92		
OCT 1 4 1997		
OCT 1 6 1997		
OCT 2 6 1998		

Victoria and Albert

Then you must also remember, that endless false and untrue things have been written and said about us, public and private, and that in these days people will write and will know; therefore the only way to counteract this is to let the real, full truth be known, and as much be told as can be told with prudence and discretion, and then no harm, but good, will be done. Nothing will help me more than that my people should see what I have lost.

Queen Victoria to Princess Alice,
on the publication of Prince Albert's biography.

VICTORIA
and
ALBERT

JOANNA RICHARDSON

Quadrangle/
The New York Times Book Co.

First published in Great Britain in 1977 by
J. M. Dent & Sons Ltd.

Library of Congress Catalog Card Number: 76-52822
International Standard Book Number: 0-8129-0692-6

Contents

Acknowledgments

The author would like to acknowledge the gracious permission of Her Majesty The Queen to reprint from various published sources a number of passages from the royal correspondence.

The author would also like to thank the following for their assistance in supplying photographic prints: the Lord Chamberlain's Office, St James's Palace, the Royal Library and Royal Archives, Windsor Castle, the Victoria & Albert Museum, the Trustees of the British Museum and the Gernsheim Collection, Humanities Research Centre, The University of Texas at Austin.

List of Photographs

List of Photographs

List of Photographs

Introduction

Since I first read English history, I have been enthralled by Queen Victoria and Prince Albert; and, re-reading the biographies, the letters, journals and memoirs, I find that the fascination remains. In the case of Prince Albert, it is true, the fascination is largely intellectual. The breadth of his achievements in the arts and social sciences and in educational reform is, by any standards, remarkable. His political significance has yet to be assessed; but, direct or indirect, it was extraordinary. He commands our admiration – but rarely our affection. He remains as foreign to us as he did to his contemporaries. He has, I suspect, suffered as much from his wife's adulation as from the nation's lasting mistrust. He is noble and philanthropic, but he is cold. He has no weakness and no passion. We cannot ever find him endearing. His nature remains enigmatic. It seems to lack humanity. And yet this stern, controlled intellectual, indifferent to women, almost devoid of humour and gusto, was married to a woman who abounded in vitality.

Vitality was one of Queen Victoria's greatest assets; and, re-reading her letters, we are swept along by it today. The government of a growing Empire, the demands of Court and society, of her husband and nine children: none of this prevented her from keeping up a voluminous correspondence, or from writing her journal every day of her long life. That Princess Beatrice destroyed the vast bulk of this journal is a major loss for the historian and a literary tragedy for us all.

Three-quarters of a century after her death, Queen Victoria still remains a presence. To her, as to thinking people today, patriotism was natural; but she expressed it in superb, inimitable style. To her, again – as to thinking people – right and wrong were sharply defined, standards were set to be maintained, and work was there to be done. Queen Victoria was liberal in her views: indeed, in many ways she was less Victorian than her contemporaries. But in one Victorian creed she firmly believed: a happy marriage was the centre of life; the family was the solid foundation of society. We may recall her belief and her example with great profit.

During the last twelve years Lady Longford has published *Victoria R. I.* and Mrs Woodham-Smith has published the first part of her life of Queen Victoria. Mr Robert Rhodes James is to write the first full-length study of the Prince Consort to appear since Sir Theodore Martin's official biography. This, therefore, is not the moment to attempt a 'definitive' account of Queen Victoria's marriage. When I was asked to write this book, I had, reluctantly, to agree on the understanding that it would be based on published works. Much of it may, therefore, be familiar to the reader; some, I hope, will be little known. But I have written of Queen Victoria with affection and, in general, with admiration.

I must also record my debt to previous biographers: especially to E. F. Benson, for his *Queen Victoria*, and to Mr Roger Fulford, for his life of the Prince Consort, and for his edition of Queen Victoria's correspondence with her eldest daughter. I owe much to Mrs Woodham-Smith's authoritative work.

Joanna Richardson 1977

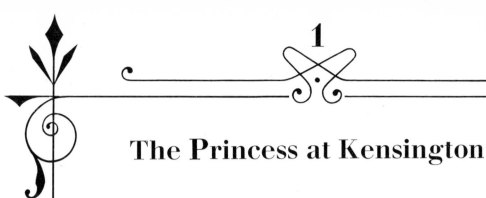

The Princess at Kensington

Kings and Queens satisfy the need of common man for heroes. They are the symbols of our nationhood; they are also the embodiment of traditions which transcend our daily politics. Ideally they represent the continuity of history. The Commonwealth of Oliver Cromwell lasted a decade; the British Monarchy has lasted for over a thousand years, and even the Abdication of Edward VIII, forty years ago, ultimately served to strengthen it. The fact that the British Monarchy so strongly endures owes much to Queen Victoria. 'They say', she wrote, 'that no Sovereign was ever loved more than I am, and *this* because of our happy domestic home, and the good example it presents.' The statement was self-satisfied, it was sanctimonious, and it was undoubtedly true.

When Queen Victoria came to the throne on 20 June 1837, the monarchy was in a parlous state. The Hanoverians had not served it well. The first two Georges had insisted, defiantly, on their German sympathies, and they had not even spoken English. George I had suspected his wife, Sophia Dorothea, of a love-affair with Königsmarck, and he had imprisoned her for life. George II had flaunted his mistresses in front of his Queen. George III had, admittedly, 'gloried in the name of Briton', and he had given the nation no fewer than fifteen children; but his long, contented marriage to Charlotte of Mecklenburg-Strelitz had finally been clouded by the royal malady, porphyria, and he had spent more than a decade apparently insane. As for his sons, their irregularities had been a rich and unending source of gossip. The most gifted of them, the Prince of Wales (later Regent and George IV) had been unable to make an official marriage with the woman he considered his true wife. Mrs Fitzherbert was admirable, but she was a commoner, and (which made marriage impossible) she was Catholic. Caroline of Brunswick was a princess, and she was Protestant, but she was also mentally disturbed. It is remarkable that Queen Charlotte knew Caroline's reputation for outrageous behaviour, and still allowed her son to make this marriage. But Caroline was the daughter of the King's favourite sister, Augusta, Duchess of Brunswick; and 'the fact is', so the Queen explained, 'that the King is completely ignorant of everything concerning the Duke's Family, and that it would be unseemly to speak to him against his niece.' Decorum was preserved, the Brunswick marriage had taken place, and it had been followed by continual domestic scandal. Caroline's behaviour had prompted the Delicate Investigation (an official enquiry into her conduct), and the Bill of Pains and Penalties (her trial by the House of Lords for alleged adultery with an Italian courier). As for Caroline's husband, he had made himself unpopular by his devotion to Lady Hertford and to Lady Conyngham. The only justification of his marriage was his daughter, Princess Charlotte, who had been the hope of the nation. In 1816 she had married Leopold of Saxe-Coburg; in 1817 she had died, after giving birth to a still-born son.

In the brief year of her married life with her German princeling, Princess Charlotte had offered the country what it had needed for generations: a model of royal domesticity. The thought of this handsome and virtuous young couple leading their idyllic life at Claremont, near Esher, and setting an example of restrained, correct behaviour, had been singularly warming and refreshing. One cannot regret that the daughter of Caroline of Brunswick (who was touched, perhaps, by porphyria) failed to ascend the throne. One can only be thankful that Leopold of Saxe-Coburg, interfering, cold and calculating, finally practised his science of kingship in Belgium. But when Princess Charlotte died, at the age of twenty-one, there was deep and understandable regret. It appeared all too probable that the Regent would become George IV, and that in time he would be succeeded by one of his eccentric brothers. They were all middle-aged, and none of them had legitimate offspring.

It was clear that one of them must rapidly produce an heir to the throne. This duty was plain to Edward, Duke of Kent. The Duke, an ex-soldier, was fifty, and since he was twenty-three he has been living happily with his French mistress, Madame Saint-Laurent. Since he was in debt to the tune of some £50,000, he had made his home in Brussels with Madame Saint-Laurent and his equerry, Captain John Conroy. It was in Brussels that he learned of his niece's death; and in Brussels he chose to unbosom himself to an ex-Member of Parliament, the untiring and useful diarist Thomas Creevey. Mr Creevey at once recorded the royal conversation. Posterity must be grateful for the Duke's indiscretion and for Mr Creevey's diligence.

The Regent (said the Duke of Kent) would not have another heir, for in order to get one he would have to divorce his wife. Her adultery, if proved, would be equivalent to high treason, and it would be punishable by death. It was, therefore, certain (here the Duke was wrong) that the Regent would not attempt divorce. As for Frederick, Duke of York, his wife was now too old to have a child. William, Duke of Clarence, would demand not only a handsome settlement, but the payment of his massive debts and a generous provision for each of the ten FitzClarences – his children by the actress Mrs Jordan. The fourth brother in the order of succession was himself; and although, he said, 'I trust I shall be at all times ready to obey any call my country might make upon me, God only knows the sacrifice it will be to make it, whenever I shall think it my duty to become a married man.' Madame Saint-Laurent was already distraught at the very notion, but the Duke had drawn up his plan of action. He would give his brother William three months; if during that time William took no steps towards matrimony, the Duke had determined to go to England, and to 'take measures' himself.

The year 1818 brought some savage comments on the royal brothers, their respective states of health, and their prospects of fruitful marriage. As St George's Day approached (it was now the Regent's official birthday), even Sir Robert Peel, who was more tolerant of royalty than most, professed himself astonished by the wild behaviour of the Prime Minister. Lord Liverpool had proposed to give increased allowances to the royal dukes to promote their marriages. How, enquired Peel, could Lord Liverpool expect Parliament to grant an extra £12,000 a year to the

The Duke of Kent, Queen Victoria's father. Miniature after a painting by Sir William Beechey, c. 1818. Copyright reserved.

Duke of Cumberland? It was now two years since his marriage to Princess Frederica of Mecklenburg-Strelitz, and in the interval his dress and manner had become 'ten times more germanized than they were before . . ., his beard, whiskers and mustachios making a daily increase of their dominions.' The Duke of Wellington was still more outspoken. When the ubiquitous Mr Creevey had dined with him at Cambrai on 17 July, they discussed the future of the Regent's brothers. 'By God!' snapped Wellington, 'there is a great deal to be said about that. They are the damnedest millstone about the necks of any Government that can be imagined!'

The royal dukes had at least been determined to do their dynastic duty. Four days earlier, on Monday, 13 July, in Queen Charlotte's drawing-room at Kew Palace, the Duke of Clarence, aged fifty-three, had been united to a bride 'with hair of a peculiar colour approaching to a lemon tint, weak eyes and a bad complexion': Princess Adelaide of Saxe-Meiningen. The Duke of

Kent, aged fifty-one, had become the lawful husband of Victoria Mary Louisa of Saxe-Coburg. The new Duchess of Kent – aged thirty-two – was the widow of Emich Charles, Prince of Leiningen. She was also the sister of Prince Leopold; and years later, after her death, a letter from Leopold was found among her papers. It was dated 1818, and it urged the Duke of Kent to marry her.

Twice within two years, this family of German princelings had been summoned to ensure the future of the English monarchy. From this little duchy, Saxe-Coburg, which much resembled Pumpernickel in *Vanity Fair*, there was to rise an astonishing dynasty. On 24 May 1819, the Duke of Kent was rewarded for his patriotic marriage by the birth of 'a pretty little Princess, as plump as a partridge'. She was christened Alexandrina Victoria.

Three months after Frau Siebold, the midwife, had performed her duties at Kensington Palace, she was summoned to the Rosenau, about four miles from the town of Coburg. It was a summer residence of Duke Ernest of Saxe-Coburg, brother of Leopold and the Duchess of Kent. On 26 August the Duchess Louise, who was only nineteen, was delivered of her second son: Francis Albert Augustus Charles Emmanuel. The day after Albert's birth his grandmother, the Dowager Duchess, announced the event to her daughter the Duchess of Kent; and, alluding to the month in which Princess Victoria had been born, she added: 'How pretty the *May Flower* will be when I see her in a year's time! Siebold cannot say often enough what a dear little love she is.'

In the meanwhile, on 24 June, the Mayflower had been christened in a gold font brought from the Tower of London. The ceremony had taken place at Kensington Palace, where her parents kept up a modest Royal Household; their finances were strained by the arrival of Princess Feodora of Leiningen, the Duchess's daughter by her previous marriage, and by the arrival of Feodora's governess, Fraulein Lehzen. Debts continued to accumulate, and the Duke – who was now in a strong dynastic position – even threatened to leave England and live in Leiningen, unless the Regent came to his rescue.

There was no time for such a move. In December, the Kents took Woolbrook Cottage at Sidmouth in Devonshire to escape the winter fogs of London, and at Sidmouth tragedy befell them. The winter of 1819–20 was exceptionally hard; there were fierce storms, gales and glacial cold. The Kents arrived at Sidmouth on the afternoon of Christmas Day in the midst of a tremendous snowstorm. The Duke caught a chill and developed pneumonia. At times he was delirious. The doctors tried to lower the fever; they bled him to the point of exhaustion. He had made a will appointing his equerry, Captain Conroy, as an executor, and appointing the Duchess as sole guardian of his child. Now he summoned up his remaining strength and signed it. On 23 January he died.

He was only fifty-three; and, as John Wilson Croker, the Tory politician, observed, he had been 'the strongest of the strong; . . . and now to die of a cold,' added Croker, 'when half the kingdom has colds with impunity, is very bad luck indeed'. However, the Duke had happily ensured the succession. And, within a week of his death, the succession to the throne assumed a sudden and increased importance. On the evening of 29 January, in the eighty-second year of his age, 'without any appearance of pain and without a lucid interval', King George III died, at long last, at Windsor. On 31 January, George IV was proclaimed King of England.

Even before the Duke of Kent had died, Prince Leopold had hurried down from Claremont to his sister. George IV would have been very glad to see her depart with her infant daughter, and indeed the Duchess would readily have returned to Leiningen to resume her regency for her son Charles – now sixteen – and to bring up Victoria abroad. Leopold insisted that she must stay in England, and the Duchess abandoned the thought of her regency. On the day of her husband's death, she left 'melancholy Sidmouth', and returned to London with her daughter Feodora – aged twelve – and the baby of eight months. The principal members of her household were her lady-in-waiting, Baroness Spaeth, her daughter's governess, Louise Lehzen, and, as secretary and controller of her household, the Duke's equerry and executor, Captain Conroy. The Captain had a wife and several children. They settled into somewhat restricted quarters at Kensington Palace. Here the Duchess and Victoria were to live for seventeen years.

The Duchess of Kent had been devoted to her second husband.
Years later, when Queen Victoria was obliged to sort her
mother's papers, she was moved to find 'how very very much
she and my beloved Father *loved* each other. *Such* love and
affection! I hardly knew it was *to that extent*'. But when the Duke
died, the Duchess had been only thirty-three; and, isolated by
widowhood, by her status, by her loneliness in a foreign country, she came increasingly under the influence of Captain Conroy. He was Irish, good-looking and ambitious: a disappointed
man who suddenly saw a prospect of boundless glory. The
Duchess of Kent had sole charge of the child who would one day
become Queen of England. It was quite possible that Victoria
would ascend the throne before she came of age, and that a
regency would be necessary. If the Duchess of Kent were
Regent, Conroy – the equerry – might make himself the power
behind the throne.

The Duchess of Kent and Princess
Victoria, aged three. Painting by
Sir William Beechey, 1822.
Copyright reserved.

He did his utmost to ensure that the Duchess depended on him. The 'dear devoted friend of my Edward' became the devoted friend of Edward's widow. He soothed her well-founded anxieties about the Duke's affairs; he performed his task as executor with remarkable energy. The 'very intelligent factotum' became the indispensable friend. How intimate their relations were may never be known; but Conroy's ascendency over the Duchess, and his determination to gain ascendency over her daughter, were to determine the course of Victoria's childhood.

Conroy devised 'the Kensington System'. The system was, briefly, to isolate Victoria from the world, and to make her dependent on her mother – who, in turn, depended on himself. The system decreed that Victoria must be kept apart from all her relatives – especially from the English Royal Family. She must never be alone, day or night. She must always sleep in her mother's room, she must always walk downstairs with someone holding her hand. She must never see anyone, young or old, unless a third person were present.

Prince Leopold, as her uncle, should have prevented the imposition of this monstrous system. The Duchess of Kent, wrote Prince Albert, later, 'would never have fallen into the hands of Conroy if Uncle Leopold had taken the trouble to guide her'. But though the widowed Duchess accepted £3,000 a year from her brother, she resolutely refused to be guided by him. Conroy poisoned her mind against him, and for some time Prince Leopold withdrew from her affairs. Not until 1850 – four years before Conroy's death – did the Duchess learn how hugely Conroy had defrauded her.

In the 1820s she was only aware of his efficiency and his devotion. King George IV was persuaded, as King of Hanover, to create him a Knight Commander of the Hanoverian Order, so that he became Sir John Conroy. Sir John encouraged the Duchess to isolate Kensington Palace from the world. Princess Feodora, her elder daughter, later told Queen Victoria: 'When I look back upon those years which ought to have been the happiest in my life, . . . I cannot help pitying myself. Not to have enjoyed the pleasures of youth is nothing, but to have been deprived of all intercourse and not one cheerful thought in that dismal existence of ours, was very hard. My only happy time was going or driving out with you and Lehzen; then I could speak and look as I liked.' In 1826 Conroy told the Duchess that Princess Feodora should marry soon. 'It is necessary for yours and the Pss. Victoria's interest that [the marriage] should take place – the influence you ought to have over [Princess Victoria] will be endangered if she sees an older sister not so alive to it as she should be – and recollect, once your authority is lost over the Princess V you will never regain it. . . .' In 1828 Princess Feodora was duly married to Prince Ernest Christian Charles of Hohenlohe-Langenburg. The marriage was not brilliant, but Conroy had recommended it to the Duchess. Feodora did not marry for love, but to get away from life at Kensington Palace. 'I escaped some years of imprisonment, which you, my poor Sister, had to endure after I was married', she wrote to Queen Victoria in 1843. 'Often I have praised God that he sent my dearest Ernest, for I might have married I don't know whom – merely to get away.'

So Feodora married and crossed the Channel, and Victoria returned to the dolls who were her essential companions. She felt an aversion to Conroy, and she could not feel close to her mother. Only her governess, Louise Lehzen, earned her love and trust. George IV had raised Lehzen to the rank of a Hanoverian Baroness. 'She never for the 13 years she was governess to Pss Victoria, *once left her*', Queen Victoria was to write, '. . . and knew how to amuse and play with the Princess so as to gain her warmest affections. The Princess was her only object and her only thought. She was very strict and the Pss. had great respect and even awe of her, but with that the greatest affection. . . .'

Victoria's emotional life was deliberately restricted; but her education became extensive. Mrs Anderson – a pupil of Mendelssohn – taught her the piano. Mr Sale, the organist at St Margaret's, Westminster, taught her singing (she had a sweet contralto voice). Richard Westall, of the Royal Academy, instructed her in drawing. Mlle Bourdin showed her how to dance the minuet, and Monsieur Grandineau helped her to speak French. She spoke German, of course (the German accent had to be eliminated from her English). She struggled to learn English grammar from Mr Steward of Westminster School. It was, again, Mr Steward who taught her arithmetic, for which she had a particular talent. The general supervisor of her studies was the Reverend George Davys, later Dean of Chester and Bishop of

Peterborough. He had begun her instruction when she was four years old, and he respected her abilities. Victoria herself did not. 'I was not', she remembered, 'fond of learning as a little child – and baffled every attempt to teach me my letters up to 5 years old – when I consented to learn them'.

Perhaps, before she was ten, she already understood her future. Sir Walter Scott suspected that 'if we could dissect the little heart, we should find that some pigeon or other bird of the air had carried the matter'. Baroness Lehzen – 'sagacious Baroness Lehzen', some called her – claimed that, when Victoria was eleven, she had slipped a Royal Family tree into her history book; the child had understood, and said: 'I will be good.' The legend is endearing, but Victoria herself thought that it was not entirely true. However, nobody could deny her instinctive goodness; and Mr Creevey, who saw her in a box at the Opera, decided that 'she looked a very nice little girl indeed'.

The prospect of Victoria was, even now, refreshing; and it was already very near. Frederick Duke of York had died in 1827, George IV – 'dear Uncle King' – died in 1830, and only William IV now stood between Victoria and the throne. The Duchess of Kent underlined the fact by taking her daughter on royal progresses round her future kingdom. The Heiress Apparent was well received, but William IV was understandably annoyed by the Duchess's behaviour. The Duchess made no secret of her antagonism towards him. Their skirmishes were even less restrained when, in 1831, Prince Leopold accepted the crown of Belgium, and could not so easily influence his sister.

But influence he intended to keep. He sat at the cross-roads of politics; and he maintained a constant correspondence with his niece. He intended to form her political views and her moral standards. He also intended to arrange her marriage. He had of course chosen her husband for her.

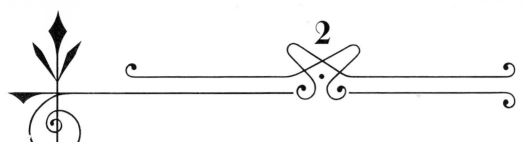

The Coburg Marriage

The House of Saxe-Coburg was one of the many branches of the ancient House of Wettin. Since the eleventh century they had ruled over Meissen and the territory around it, and to these domains had been added Upper Saxony and Thuringia. In the fifteenth century all the possessions of the House had been divided between the two great branches, the Albertine and the Ernestine. The Albertine branch kept Meissen and the Saxon possessions. They held the title of Elector, which they exchanged in 1806 for that of King. The Ernestine branch ruled over Thuringia, but, according to the common German custom, it had again broken up into many branches, and the duchies of Thuringia were divided among them. On the extinction of the Gotha line, in 1826, the family property was rearranged, and the Duke of Saxe-Coburg was given Gotha. Thanks to this constant division and subdivision, the Ernestine princes exercised no influence in German affairs. In Coburg, in the heart of Germany, hedged in by the Thuringian mountains, every Coburger was forced to depend on his industry and his determination.

At the end of the eighteenth century, the ducal family consisted of the ruling Duke, his three sons and four daughters. They were all poor and ambitious. Duke Francis died in 1806, and left them to fend for themselves. 'Without meaning', wrote the youngest son, 'to say anything unkind of the Saxon family, ours was more truly intelligent and more naturally so'. Queen Victoria's uncle, the Duke of Cumberland, expressed the same truth with less flattery. 'The spirit of intrigue', he said, 'exists in the whole breed'.

Whether they were intelligent or merely bent on intrigue, they recognized that their future must depend on judicious marriage. The first son of Duke Francis to marry was Prince Ferdinand. He captured Antoinette de Kohary, the heiress of one of the richest families in Hungary. He himself was Protestant, and she was Catholic, but the vast Kohary estates and the fabulous Kohary fortune were enough to lure him into the Roman Catholic Church. His descendants were to sit on the thrones of Portugal and Bulgaria. A few weeks later, Prince Leopold, the youngest of the Coburgs, made the most dazzling marriage of all. He became the husband of Princess Charlotte, the heiress to the throne of England. Although she died within eighteen months, he was left with a handsome English house and a handsome English annuity. Deprived of his royal hopes in England, he rejected the throne of Greece, and in 1831 he accepted the brand-new throne of Belgium. The following year he made a useful second marriage with Princess Louise, the daughter of Louis-Philippe, King of the French. Leopold's descendants were to reign in Belgium, his daughter married the Emperor of Mexico, his grand-daughter the heir to the Austro-Hungarian Empire, and his great-grand-daughter the heir to the throne of Italy.

The marriages of the four Coburg daughters were not always so distinguished, but they still brought lustre to the family. The eldest, Sophia, married Emmanuel, Count Mensdorff-Pouilly ('he had been no prince', a biographer explained, 'only a French emigrant officer in the Austrian service'). The second daughter, Antoinette, married Alexander, Duke of Wurtemberg. The third daughter, Julia, became the wife of the Grand Duke Constantine of Russia. The youngest, Victoria, as we have seen, married Emich Charles, Prince of Leiningen, and, after his death, the Duke of Kent.

The last of the Coburgs to marry was the head of the family. In 1817 Duke Ernest, the reigning Duke, married Princess Louise of Saxe-Gotha-Altenburg. Their elder son, Ernest, was born in 1818; their younger son, Albert, the following year.

Louise was only seventeen when she married; and her husband was sixteen years older than herself. He was also incapable of fidelity. She was left largely to her own devices, and she was vivacious and charming. Some years after the birth of her sons, when she had been made miserable by her husband's neglect and

Louise, Duchess of Saxe-Coburg and Gotha, mother of Prince Albert. German School, 1820. Copyright reserved.

unfaithfulness, she fell in love with an officer in the Coburg army. In 1824 Duke Ernest got a separation, and the Duchess left Coburg. Her children never saw her again. In March 1826 Duke Ernest finally divorced her, on the grounds of her adultery with Lieutenant von Hanstein. She neither denied nor admitted the charge, but, seven months later, she married von Hanstein, and he was created Count von Polzig. She died of cancer at St Wendel, in Switzerland, on 31 August 1831. She was thirty-one. Prince Albert, wrote Queen Victoria, never forgot his mother, 'and spoke with much tenderness and sorrow of her, and was deeply affected in reading, after his marriage, the accounts of her sad and painful illness. One of the first gifts he made to the Queen was a little pin he had received from her when a little child.' Years after the Duchess died, her remains were taken back to Coburg, and interred in the family mausoleum. In the autumn of 1860, Queen Victoria laid a wreath on her tomb.

Before he was five years old, Prince Albert was motherless. But, though his mother had gone, he was not deprived of feminine influence. His grandmother, the Dowager Duchess of Saxe-Coburg, lavished affection on him; so did his mother's step-mother, the Duchess of Saxe-Gotha-Altenburg. In 1832 Duke Ernest married his niece, Princess Marie of Wurtemberg, and this second marriage ensured that there was still a gentle presence in Prince Albert's life. As a man, he often told the Queen – with a certain want of tact – that his childhood had been the happiest period of his whole existence.

He was a remarkably pretty child, with fair hair and his mother's blue eyes. 'The Prince', wrote an observer, later, 'bears a striking resemblance to his mother, and at the same time, though differing in much, takes after her in many respects, both physical and mental. He has the same mobility and readiness of mind, and the same intelligence, the same over-ruling desire and talent for appearing kind and amiable to others, the same tendency to *espièglerie*, to treat things and people in a droll and often amusing fashion, the same habit of not dwelling long on a subject.'

This gaiety, this butterfly nature were later to vanish, and a deep earnestness was to take their place; but in many things Albert was to remain very like his mother. He was also, in much, to be feminine by nature. Even as a baby, he disliked being tended by women, and when he was three he was taken from his nurse, and handed over to Herr Florschütz, who remained his tutor until he was eighteen. 'Albert adores his Uncle Leopold', his mother had written before the separation. 'He gazes at him, and he is always kissing him.' Already, it seems, Albert preferred a masculine presence. His mistrust of women was finally confirmed when his mother left him. To any child the experience would be deeply disturbing; to Albert, one suspects, it did lasting damage.

At the age of six, he began to keep a diary, which reads like that of a hypersensitive girl. 'We recited, and I cried because I could not say my repetition, for I had not paid attention. . . . I wrote a letter at home. But because I had made so many mistakes in it, the Rath [Herr Florschütz] tore it up, and threw it into the fire. I cried about it. . . .' There was hardly a day without weeping or repentance. Once, it is true, he was tough enough to fight his elder brother; but, alas, even then he was sorry for the offence.

Marie, Duchess of Saxe–Coburg and Gotha, stepmother of Prince Albert. German School. Copyright reserved.

At last an unexpected, more robust streak appeared in his nature. He proved to be an excellent mimic. He also showed a taste for practical jokes. He persuaded his chemistry tutor to fill a number of small glass bulbs with sulphuretted hydrogen; he dropped these into the pit in the Coburg theatre, and laughed uncontrollably when they burst and filled the auditorium with their stench. One of his cousins put on her cloak after a visit to the ducal palace. She found the pockets stuffed with soft cheese. She retaliated, rightly, by filling Albert's bed with frogs. He was not amused.

Then Albert's schoolboy gaiety was suddenly forgotten in a passion for self-improvement. At the age of thirteen he drew up a daunting time-table for his lessons. They began at six every morning, and occupied six hours a day. When he was fifteen, he and his brother were confirmed together. The day before the ceremony, the Court chaplain gave them a *viva voce* examination in theology. It took place in the presence of a host of relatives, Court and government officials, and deputations from surrounding towns and villages. It lasted for an hour, and both princes gave great satisfaction.

Whatever satisfaction they gave, and whatever Queen Victoria later declared for the benefit of her subjects, the truth was that Prince Albert was not religious. He was bored by theology. Piety as meaning reverence for God was a piety he never understood. Prince Albert believed in the life after death and in a beneficent Creator. But his religious opinions were unorthodox. He had, in time, to be warned to be more circumspect in his criticisms of the Church of England; and Lady Ponsonby, the wife of one of his secretaries, bluntly observed: 'Churchmen could not but distrust him.'

However, such unorthdoxy could not be foreseen at his confirmation. When the ceremony was over, he and his brother visited a number of relations. Then they returned to Coburg and resumed their studies until, in the spring of 1836, their father took them to England.

It is clear from the letters which she wrote this year to King Leopold, that Princess Victoria knew the destiny which he intended for her. William IV knew it, too, and he disapproved. Leopold and the Duchess of Kent had given him a natural distaste

Princess Victoria, aged sixteen, an
her spaniel Dash. Portrait by Sir
George Hayter, 1835.

for the opportunist and brazen Coburgs. He wanted his niece to marry Alexander, the younger son of William, Prince of Orange.

Leopold had arranged that his brother Ernest should bring his two sons, Ernest and Albert, to stay with their aunt, the Duchess of Kent, at Kensington Palace. They were to come in May. A day or two before they started, Leopold received a half-official communication from England saying that it would be '*highly desirable*' that this Coburg visit should not take place. In the meanwhile, King William had invited the Prince of Orange and his sons to Windsor.

Leopold was shaken. He wrote his niece such an angry letter that he thought it wise to entrust it to a special messenger.

> I am [he said] really *astonished* at the conduct of your old Uncle the King; this invitation of the Prince of Orange and his sons, this forcing him upon others, is very extraordinary. . . .
>
> I have not the least doubt that the King, in his passion for the Oranges, will be *excessively rude to your relations*; this, however, will not signify much; they are *your guests* and not *his*, and will therefore *not* mind it.

The Prince of Orange and his sons had in fact arrived already; and, that day, the King and Queen gave a ball in their honour at St James's Palace. Victoria was present. 'I shall . . . give you an account of the Oranges, whom we have the dissatisfaction of having here.' So she reported to King Leopold. 'The Prince . . . I think looks put out [and] embarrassed, particularly so with us. The boys are both very plain and have a mixture of Kalmuck and Dutch in their faces, moreover they look heavy, dull and frightened and are not at all prepossessing. So much for the *Oranges*, dear Uncle.'

Five days after the Orange ball, the Saxe-Coburgs made their triumphant appearance at Kensington.

> My dearest Uncle [Victoria wrote],
>
> . . . Uncle Ernest and my cousins arrived here on Wednesday, *sains et saufs*. Uncle is looking remarkably well, and my cousins are most delightful young people. . . . They are both very amiable, very kind and good, and extremely merry, just as young people should be; with all that, they are extremely sensible, and very fond of occupation. Albert is extremely handsome. . . .

Victoria and her cousins - and, no doubt, the vigilant Duchess
– went to the Opera to hear *Il Puritani*; Albert and Ernest proved
to be 'excessively fond of music, like me', and 'they were in
perfect ecstasies'. Victoria, too, was in ecstasies, for Albert, with
his dark brown hair, fine features, and large blue eyes, was as
handsome as a prince in legend. They were still almost children:
her seventeenth birthday fell soon after her cousins arrived.
Albert was to be seventeen in August. But even now, when she
first set eyes on the prince whom politics had chosen for her,
Victoria was in love with her destiny.

The Duchess of Kent did not intend that the destiny should be
forgotten. On her daughter's birthday she presented Albert with
a ring. The name Victoria was engraved on it.

The welcome was effusive, the hopes and plans were evident,
but Albert did not feel overjoyed. He was delicate, he was
already subject to rheumatism and gastric attacks; late hours did
not suit him. Besides, he was still unhappy in women's company. He was embarrassed to be sent to London 'on approval' for
Victoria; and he did not feel at home in England.

Dear Mama [he wrote to his stepmother on 1 June],

Accept mine and Ernest's heartfelt thanks for your. dear, kind
letter. I would have answered you sooner if I had not been suffering
for some days from a bilious fever. The climate of this country, the
different way of living, and the late hours, do not agree with me. I
am, however, fairly upon my legs again.

My first appearance was at a levée of the King's which was long
and fatiguing, but very interesting. The same evening we dined at
Court, and at night there was a beautiful concert, at which we had to
stand till two o'clock. The next day, the King's birthday was kept.
We went in the middle of the day to a Drawing-room at St James's
Palace, at which about 3,800 people passed before the King and
Queen and the other high dignitaries, to offer their congratulations.
There was again a great dinner in the evening, and then a concert
which lasted till one o'clock. You can well imagine that I had many
hard battles fo fight against sleepiness. . . .

The day before yesterday, our Aunt gave a brilliant ball here at
Kensington Palace, at which the gentlemen appeared in uniform, and
the ladies in so-called fancy dresses. We remained till four o'clock....

Dear Aunt is very kind to us, and does everything she can to please
us; and our cousin also is very amiable.

It was not the language of love.

Victoria herself remained in ecstasies. Here, at last, was youthful company; here, at last, was a sign that her melancholy childhood would one day end, and that she might enjoy a delightful future. When, after three weeks at Kensington, her cousins were obliged to depart, Duke Ernest took King Leopold an entirely satisfactory letter. 'I must thank you, my beloved Uncle, for the prospect of *great* happiness you have contributed to give me in the person of dear Albert. Allow me, then, my dearest Uncle, to tell you how delighted I am with him in every way. He possesses every quality that could be desired to make me perfectly happy.'

Years later, she told Prince Albert's biographer that 'she never had an idea, if she married at all, of anyone else'.

After the fatigues of London, Albert was perfectly content to settle down with his brother and Herr Florschütz in Brussels, and to pursue his academic studies. In Brussels they remained for nearly a year. In the spring of 1837 they moved on to Bonn University, 'in search of more wisdom'. They attended lectures on law, on the science of government, on history, philosophy, literature and the history of art. They were driven by what Ernest called 'reading mania'. Albert loved university life. In those days it was untainted by the presence of women. When his father invited him and Ernest to Coburg for Christmas, Albert refused. His course of study must not be disturbed.

King Leopold, however, was always vigilant, always aware of Albert's destiny. He recognized that academic life was unlikely to encourage thoughts of matrimony. He and his confidential agent, Baron Stockmar, therefore decided that Albert should visit Italy. His appreciation of Italy and Italian women must, none the less, be kept within bounds by the company of Stockmar and a young English officer, Lieutenant Seymour. Sir Francis Seymour, as he became, did his best to preserve the purity of Albert's life. But Albert was not tempted by women. From Florence, which he reached at the end of 1838, he wrote triumphantly to Florschütz: 'Every morning by five o'clock I sit down at my little student's lamp.' In the summer of 1839, after a visit to Rome, he returned to Coburg. He had spent six months in Italy. 'My range of observation has been doubled', he told Prince William of Löwenstein, 'and my power of forming a right judgment will be much increased'.

His boyhood and youth were over. Some might have wished that he had more humour and more gaiety: that he was, perhaps, a little more like the rest of mankind. But he was astoundingly handsome. He was extremely intelligent, widely read, and distinguished for his high principles. His lineage, his wealth and his domains were unimpressive. He was still the most desirable prince in Europe.

Once Albert had departed in the early summer of 1836, and Victoria had written her encouraging letter to King Leopold, she was ready to forget the thought of marriage. And if, on a visit to Claremont, her uncle talked over 'many important things' with her, the most urgent of them was her accession. On 24 May 1837 she was to come of age; and then, if King William died, there would be no chance of her mother's regency. Victoria would be the Queen of England.

It was clear that she would have her Ministers to guide her; it was also clear that English politics could not be the province of the King of the Belgians. None the less King Leopold was determined to be her sole adviser; and, since letters were inadequate, he sent Baron Stockmar to counsel her.

Christian Frederick Stockmar was fifty. He had been born in Coburg, and trained as a doctor, but after the peace of 1815 he had entered Leopold's service as a confidential agent. Stockmar believed that the Coburg princes could restore the fading glories of European monarchy; and he devoted his life to working for this ideal. 'A mischievous old prig', Mr Gladstone was to call him; but there is no denying that Stockmar had considerable effect on the future of the English throne. He had hovered round Claremont in the days of Leopold's marriage to Princess Charlotte (indeed, he had been at Princess Charlotte's deathbed); he had chosen Prince Albert's tutor, Florschütz, to whom the Prince attributed his disciplined mind and his horror of vice. Stockmar, with his piercing eyes and his subfusc clothes, was to hover round the Coburgs for another two decades; and to them he was to prove useful in the extreme. He had now been fully instructed by King Leopold on the correct behaviour for Victoria when she became Queen of England; and Victoria, said the King, must always consult him.

In 1837 Victoria happily came of age; the menace of a Regency had vanished. And, as Sarah Tytler wrote, in *The Life of Her Most Gracious Majesty*:

> On 24 May, at six o'clock in the morning, the Union Jack was hoisted on the summit of the old church, Kensington, and on the flagstaff at Palace Green. In the last instance the national ensign was surmounted by a white silk flag on which was inscribed in sky-blue letters 'Victoria'. . . . Soon after six o'clock the gates of Kensington Gardens were opened for the admission of the public to be present at the serenade which was to be performed at seven o'clock under the Palace windows, with the double purpose of awaking the Princess in the most agreeable manner, and of reminding her that at the same place and hour, eighteen years ago, she had opened her eyes on the May world.

She had come of age just in time to avert the disaster of a Regency. On this auspicious day, King William was already confined to his rooms at Windsor, and Queen Adelaide did not leave him. Soon afterwards it became apparent that he was dying.

> The news of the King are so very bad [recorded Victoria on 15 June], that all my lessons save the Dean's [history lesson] are put off, including Lablache's, Mrs Anderson's, . . . etc., etc., and we see *nobody*. I regret rather my singing lesson, though it is only for a short period, but duty and *proper feeling* go before all *pleasures*. . . .

Victoria already had her own standards of behaviour, her independence and determination. However, on 17 June, King Leopold sent his final instructions: 'I shall today enter on the subject of what is to be done when the King ceases to live. The moment you get official communication of it, you will entrust Lord Melbourne with the office of retaining the present Administration. . . .' It was an unbelievable letter from a foreign Head of State; but Victoria answered, tactfully: 'Stockmar has *been* and *is,* of the *greatest* possible use, and be assured, dearest Uncle, that he possesses *my most entire confidence.'*

Three days after her uncle wrote, on Tuesday, 20 June, King William died. At six o'clock that morning Victoria was woken,

and went downstairs to receive the news from the Archbishop of
Canterbury and the Lord Chamberlain. 'She came into the room
in a loose white nightgown and shawl, her nightcap thrown off,
and her hair falling upon her shoulders, her feet in slippers, tears
in her eyes, but perfectly collected and dignified.' So Miss Wynn
recorded in *Diary of a Lady of Quality*. Victoria herself recorded
that she was *alone*. The word, which she herself underlined, was
often to recur in her journals. For the whole of her life, all her
eighteen years, she had been watched, advised, accompanied.
Now the Kensington System was discarded. No one could deny
her her independence, and she asserted it from the first. Her
mother's domination was instantly over. So was her uncle's
political ambition. At half-past eight that morning, she wrote to
tell him that she was the Queen of England.

At nine o'clock she received Lord Melbourne. She saw him in
her room,

> and *of course quite alone*, as I shall *always* do all my Ministers. He kissed
> my hand, and I then acquainted him that it had long been my
> intention to retain him and the rest of the present Ministry at the head
> of affairs, and that it could not be in better hands than his. He again
> then kissed my hand. He then read to me the Declaration which I was
> to read to the Council, which he wrote himself, and which is a very
> fine one. I then talked with him some little time longer, after which
> he left me. He was in full dress. I like him very much and feel
> confidence in him. He is a very straightforward, honest, clever and
> good man.

At eleven o'clock she held a meeting of the Privy Council. 'I
went in of course', she recorded, 'quite alone . . . I was not at all
nervous and had the satisfaction of hearing that people were
satisfied with what I had done'. They were more than satisfied.
Mr Creevey decided: 'Our dear little Queen in every respect is
perfection.'

Later that day, the first of her reign, the Queen committed her
feelings to her journal.

> Since it has pleased Providence to place me in this station, I shall do
> my utmost to fulfil my duty towards my country; I am very young
> and perhaps in many, though not in all things, inexperienced, but I
> am sure that very few have more real good-will and more real desire
> to do what is fit and right than I have.

Queen Victoria receiving the news of her accession from the Lord Chamberlain, Lord Conyngham, and the Archbishop of Canterbury at Kensington Palace, 20 June 1837. Painting by H. T. Wells. Copyright reserved.

The Queen's first Privy Council. The Prime Minister, Lord Melbourne, holds the pen for the Queen to sign her Declaration. Behind and to his left is Lord Palmerston, and to his right Lord John Russell. On Lord Melbourne's left sits the Archbishop of Canterbury, next to him the Duke of Cumberland. The Duke of Wellington stands in front of the column, Sir Robert Peel next to him, and seated nearest the spectator is the Duke of Sussex. Engraving after a painting by Sir David Wilkie, 1837. Courtesy of the Trustees of the British Museum.

After dinner she saw Stockmar. He was followed by Lord Melbourne, who stayed with her for more than an hour. 'I had', she wrote, 'a very important and a very *comfortable* conversation with him'.

Leopold and Stockmar were already outmanœuvred. The Queen relied, very properly, on her Prime Minister.

Even now, Queen Victoria's character was formed. It was to mellow, but it was not to change. The loneliness of her early years, the Kensington System, to which she had resentfully submitted, had driven her into herself, and created an iron core within her. She was full of gaiety, she could enjoy herself intensely (this was, she wrote, 'the *pleasantest summer* I have ever passed in my life'); she also had an inflexible will. Once she had made a decision she would not change it, and she found decisions all the easier to make because she had a simple, straightforward mind. She had vigour, tenacity and integrity. She was not an intellectual, but she had an endless supply of common sense, and she was dedicated to her task. On 25 June she assured King Leopold: 'It is to me the *greatest pleasure* to do my duty for my country and my people, and no fatigue, however great, will be burdensome to me if it is for the welfare of the nation.'

'My dearest Cousin,' wrote Albert, from Bonn, 'now you are Queen of the mightiest land of Europe, in your hand lies the happiness of millions. May Heaven assist you and strengthen you with its strength in that high but difficult task.' Prince Albert's cousin did not find her task so difficult. From the first she revelled in her sovereignty. Mr Creevey reported that she was at work from morning to night, 'and that, even when her maid was combing out her hair, she was surrounded by official boxes and reading official papers.' Queen Victoria had the romance of youth. She was also endowed with every moral and practical qualification for her calling; and to these, from the moment of her accession, she added the instincts of a queen. She had burst from her dark, grim chrysalis: a brilliant and unexpected butterfly. She was superbly, naturally royal. Even Lord Morley, who was by no means kind about monarchs, was one day to write: 'Queen Victoria stands in the first place, for not only was her rank and station illustrious, but her personality was extraordinary.'

Queen Victoria came to the throne at the perfect moment in history. She inherited a kingdom – indeed, a growing Empire – and a monarchy which had not enjoyed much affection or respect for the previous one hundred and twenty-three years. Her personal presence was needed; and history was kind in giving her the perfect man to school her in politics. The whole of Lord Melbourne's life appeared to have been a preparation for these

Queen Victoria's Coronation, 28 June 1838 Painting by C. R. Leslie. c. 1839.

last, delightful four years. Queen Victoria needed fatherly guidance. Melbourne was nearly sixty, and he was old enough to
have been her father. He was also handsome, patrician, sophisti-
cated and charming. He was romantic and chivalrous. He could
guide her without offence because he was Prime Minister,
because he was wise, and, above all, because he was fond of her
and because she was decidedly fond of him. Queen Victoria, like
most women, was influenced by her affections. And so she not
only saw her Prime Minister daily about affairs of state, but she
invited him to dine, almost every night, she rode with him, she
recorded his conversations, and on occasion she wrote to him
two or three times a day. His presence gave her security. On 28
June 1838, the day of her Coronation, what touched her most
was the fatherly look which Lord Melbourne gave her when she
was crowned. He dined with her that evening. 'And you did it so
well: excellent!' he said, and there were tears in his eyes. After
dinner, despite the hundred guests, they had their usual talk.
Then from the roof of Buckingham Palace, the Queen watched
the grand display of fireworks in the Green Park, and the general
illumination of London.

King Leopold and his wife had not come to the Coronation,
but in September they paid a visit to the Queen at Windsor. It
must have been painfully clear to the King that Lord Melbourne
had supplanted him.

He could only hope to retrieve this loss of influence by arranging
his niece's marriage. But in the past three years, since Albert's
visit, and since she had warmly accepted her uncle's choice,
Victoria had changed. She was not merely older, she had become
Queen of England, and that had altered her values. Besides she
exulted in her new, delightful independence. She disliked the
thought of losing it.

However, her marriage had become a national concern. Albert
was known to be a candidate. The fact that he was King
Leopold's choice was not in his favour. Leopold meddled with
English affairs, he came to England too often, he had – for the
Coburgs were grasping – kept Claremont and his large annuity.
He had also married again – this time a daughter of the King of
the French. There were many reasons why Leopold was un-
popular; and in December 1838 *The Times* bluntly observed:

'There is no foreigner who sets foot in England less welcome to the people generally than Leopold Brummagem King of Belgium.' As for Prince Albert, he was, said *The Times*, 'of an untoward disposition, . . . he was intellectually and morally unfit'. Besides, Lord Melbourne did not approve of him as a possible husband. 'Cousins', he said, 'are not very good things, and these Coburgs are not popular abroad: the Russians hate them'. The Queen was in an impasse. To her, Prince Albert seemed the only available candidate, though she saw no need to marry for some years. 'I said I dreaded the thought of marrying: that I was so accustomed to have my own way that I thought it was 10 to 1 that I shouldn't agree with anybody.'

In June 1839 King Leopold suggested that Ernest and Albert should visit her. At first she wanted them to come; but in July she changed her mind again. On 12 July she discussed the whole 'odious' matter with Lord Melbourne. He agreed that seeing Albert would be very disagreeable.

> I said better wait till impatience was shown [the Queen recorded in her journal]. 'Certainly better wait for a year or two,' he said; 'it's a very serious question.' I said I wished if possible never to marry. 'I don't know about *that*', he replied. . . .

Three days later, Victoria sent King Leopold an ultimatum.

> First of all, I wish to know if *Albert* is aware of the wish of his *Father* and *you* relative to *me*? Secondly, if he knows that there is *no engagement* between us? I am anxious that you should acquaint Uncle Ernest, that if I should like Albert, that I can make *no final promise this year*, for, at the *very earliest*, any such event could not take place till *two or three years hence*. For, independent of my youth, and my great repugnance to change my present position, there is *no anxiety* evinced in *this country* for such an event, and it would be more prudent, in my opinion, to wait till some such demonstration is shown – else if I were hurried it might produce discontent.
>
> Though all the reports of Albert are most favourable, and though I have little doubt I shall like him, I may not have the *feeling* for him which is requisite to ensure happiness. I *may* like him as a friend, and as a *cousin*, and as a *brother*, but not *more*; and should this be the case (which is not likely), I am *very* anxious that it should be understood that I am *not* guilty of any breach of promise, for *I never gave any*.

King Leopold and his wife considered it prudent to pay Victoria a visit. She took no pleasure in it. She recognized her uncle, rightly, as the main contriver of this disagreeable situation.

On 3 August she and Lord Melbourne talked yet again about marriage. 'You don't marry out of reason', he said, wisely. 'You marry because you fall in love.' On 6 August they returned to the oppressive subject of Prince Albert.

> I repeated to him [wrote the Queen] that he had said he did not like the connection; he laughed, and hesitated to say anything, but upon my urging it, he said, 'I don't like it very much'. But he agreed with me, a great deal depended upon what sort of person he was; and I said much as I loved my Country and was ready to do what was for its good, still I thought my own liking was one of the principal things. 'I think you have a right to expect that', he said. 'It's a very difficult subject; I don't think a foreign Prince would be popular.' But I said I *couldn't* and wouldn't like to marry a subject, and whatever family he belonged to, Lord M. said, they would be an object of jealousy. 'No, I don't think it would do', he added. I said I heard Albert's praises on all sides, and that he was very handsome.

Her cousins had been due to arrive at Windsor on 30 September. On 25 September Victoria decided to postpone the visit.

> My dear Uncle,
>   You will, I think, laugh when you get this letter, and will think I only mean to employ you in *stopping* my relations at Brussels, but I think you will approve of my wish. In the first place I don't think one can *reckon* on the Cousins arriving here on the 20th. Well, all I want is that *you* should detain them one or two days longer, in order that they may arrive here on *Thursday, the 3rd*, if possible *early*. My reason for this is as follows: a number of the Ministers are coming down here on Monday to stay till Thursday, on affairs of great importance, and as you know that people are always on the alert to make remarks, I think if *all* the Ministers were to be down here when they arrive, people would say – it was to *settle matters*. At all events it is better to avoid this. I think indeed a day or two at Brussels will do these young gentlemen good, and they can be properly fitted out there for their visit.
>
> Ever yours devotedly,
Victoria R.

The tone was imperious for a girl of twenty; but when Albert wrote to her to postpone the visit further, Victoria was far from satisfied. For the first time the alarming thought occurred to her that he was as reluctant as herself. 'The *retard* of these young people', she told her uncle, 'puts me rather out . . . I don't think they exhibit much *empressement* to come here, which rather shocks me.'

At last, however, the cousins set out, and on Thursday, 10 October, an apprehensive Queen sent an equerry and two carriages to meet them on their landing at the Tower of London.

Happily neither Victoria nor Albert knew the other's thoughts as the two brothers made their way to Windsor. After Prince Albert's death, in a remarkable memorandum, the Queen recorded that she could not think 'without indignation against herself, of her wish to keep the Prince waiting for probably three or four years, at the risk of ruining all his prospects for life, until she might feel inclined to marry! And the Prince has since told her that he came over in 1839 with the intention of telling her that if she could not then make up her mind, she must understand that he could not now wait for a decision, as he had done when this marriage was first talked about. The only excuse the Queen can make for herself is the fact that the sudden change from the secluded life at Kensington to the independence of her position as Queen Regnant, at the age of eighteen, put all ideas of marriage out of her mind, which she now most bitterly repents.'

On Thursday, 10 October 1839, at half-past seven, Prince Albert and his brother arrived at Windsor. At the top of the great staircase, Queen Victoria received them. 'It was', she wrote, 'with some emotion that I beheld Albert – who is *beautiful*.'

Presumably the cousins had been 'fitted out' in Brussels; but, in the dreadful crossing from Antwerp, their luggage had been delayed. Since they had no formal dress, they could not appear at a formal dinner. However, as the Queen explained to her uncle, two days later, they made their appearance after dinner 'in their *négligé*. Ernest', she wrote, 'is grown quite handsome; Albert's *beauty* is *most striking*, and he so amiable and unaffected – in short, very *fascinating*; he is excessively admired here.' He was indeed 'so excessively handsome, such beautiful blue eyes, an exquisite nose, such a pretty mouth with delicate mustachios and slight but very slight whiskers; a beautiful figure, broad in the shoulders and a fine waist.' He enjoyed music 'excessively', and he danced quadrilles to perfection.

On 13 October the Queen told Melbourne that she had 'a good deal changed' her opinions about marriage. Melbourne did not hurry her, but he understood.

'You would take another week', said Lord M.; 'certainly a very fine young man, very good-looking', in which I most readily agreed, and said he was so amiable and good-tempered, and that I had such a bad temper; of my being the 1st now to own the advantage of beauty, which Lord M. said smiling he had told me was not to be despised.

Indeed it was not to be despised. Next day the Queen informed Lord Melbourne that she had decided to marry Prince Albert.

'You have?' he said; 'well, then, about the time?' Not for a year, I thought; which he said was too long; that Parliament must be assembled in order to make provision for him, and that if it was settled 'it shouldn't be talked about,' said Lord M.; 'it prevents any objections, though I don't think there'll be much; on the contrary,' he continued with tears in his eyes, 'I think it'll be very well received; for I hear there is an anxiety now that it should be; and I'm very glad of it; I think it is a very good thing, and you'll be much more comfortable; for a woman cannot stand alone for long, in whatever situation she is. . . .' Then I asked, if I hadn't better tell Albert of my decision soon, in which Lord M. agreed.

It did not occur to either of them that Albert might need to make his own decision – or that he might refuse to marry her. On 15 October, at about half-past twelve, the Queen summoned him to a private audience, and told him 'it would make me *too happy* if he would consent to what I wished'. They were engaged. 'I feel', she wrote, 'the happiest of human beings.'

Certain people had to be told, at once, in confidence, of the engagement. Others must not learn of it until the Queen herself had made a Declaration to the Privy Council. She and the Prince had therefore to behave as if no betrothal had taken place. The King of the Belgians was, of course, among the first to learn of the event. The Queen sat down that day to write to him.

My dearest Uncle,
 . . . My mind is quite made up – and I told Albert this morning of it; the warm affection he showed me on learning this gave me *great*

pleasure. He seems *perfection*, and I think that I have the prospect of very great happiness before me. . . .

The Queen had recently told Stockmar that she did not intend to marry for some time. Now the Baron, too, must be told that she was engaged. She was disarmingly embarrassed. 'I *do* feel so guilty, I know not how to begin my letter – but . . . Albert has completely won my heart.'

Albert, too, was very happy. 'Dearest, greatly beloved Victoria,' he wrote to her, '. . . how is it that I have deserved so much love, so much affection? I cannot get used to the reality of all that I see and hear, and have to believe that Heaven has sent me an angel whose brightness shall illumine my life. Oh, that I may succeed in making you very, very happy, as happy as you deserve to be!'

Prince Albert was touched and overwhelmed. He felt the most profound affection for his future wife. But the Queen was completely in love, and Albert was not. The Queen was intensely demonstrative, and Albert was not. The Queen was enraptured by the prospect of her marriage. Albert saw that he must bid farewell to Germany and to his family, and spend the rest of his life in a foreign country. The hypothetical future which he had long considered was now to become reality. He had to summon all his sense of duty, all his principles of philanthropy. 'Apart from my relations with [Victoria]', so he told his stepmother on 5 November, 'my future position will have certain dark sides, and the skies above me will not always be blue and unclouded. Still, life, wherever one is, has its storms, and it is a support to one to feel that one has used all one's endeavours and strength in some great object, decisive for the welfare of so many.' Four days later he poured out his feelings to his usual confidant:

Dear Baron Stockmar,
   . . . Your prophecy is fulfilled. The event has come upon us by surprise, sooner than we could have expected. . . .
   I have laid to heart your friendly and kind-hearted advice as to the true foundation on which my future happiness must rest, and it agrees entirely with the principles of action which I had already privately framed for myself. An individuality, a character, which shall win the respect, the love, and the confidence of the Queen and of the nation, must be the groundwork of my position. . . .

Coburg.
From an old print.

I will not let my courage fail. With firm resolution and true zeal on my part, I cannot fail to continue 'noble, manly, and princely' in all things.

On 11 November, writing to the Dowager Duchess of Coburg, Albert revealed his apprehensions. 'Oh, the future! Does it not bring with it the moment when I shall have to take leave of my

dear, dear home, and of you! I cannot think of that without deep melancholy taking possession of me.'

These are strange letters for the man who was about to marry the most eligible woman in the world. But Albert had no need of marriage. He would have been content with a purely intellectual life. He was now to abandon his much-loved academic pursuits, and to marry a girl who had no pretentions to intellect. He was to be a stranger in an alien and, to him, barbaric land. This marriage had always seemed to him his inescapable destiny, his duty.

The cousins stayed at Windsor for a month. On 14 November they set out for Coburg. The Queen, enchanted, plunged into all the official preliminaries to her marriage.

A certain secrecy had been maintained until the Queen could announce her coming marriage to the Privy Council. Even the Duchess of Kent had not been informed, for she was known to be indiscreet. Besides, the Queen was '*brouillée* with my poor mother – so as to be almost at that time at enmity with her'. However, on 10 November, after consultation with Prince Albert, the Queen had sent for her. 'When she came, I said to her, I was going to tell her something which I was sure would please her, namely that I had chosen Albert to be my future husband; she took me in her arms and cried, and said, though I had not asked her, still that she gave her best blessing to it, and seemed delighted. . . . I sent for dearest Albert, whom she embraced and said it made her so happy, that she was as anxious for his happiness as for mine. . . .'

Whatever precautions had been taken, rumour was in the air. Expectation was already abroad. On 6 November, Lady Cowper, Melbourne's sister, had returned from a visit to Windsor to report that Prince Albert of Coburg, 'of whom there is so much talk, is a very charming young man, very well manner'd, and handsome, and gay, and said to be very well informed and sensible, so that I don't think she can find a better person to marry; tho' there is nothing declared or I believe settled at present, . . . still I think it will be sooner or later.' On 15 November, the day after the Prince's departure, Lord Melbourne instructed Mr Greville, Clerk to the Privy Council, to search the Council books for the form of declaration of the

Sovereign's marriage. 'So that matter', observed Mr Greville, 'is pretty clearly settled.' That day the Queen wrote to all the Royal Family, and announced her decision to them. On 21 November she explained to her fiancé:

> It is desired here that the matter should be declared at Coburg as soon as possible, and immediately after that I shall send you the Order [of the Garter].
> *Your rank will be settled just before you come over, as also your rank in the Army.* Everything will be very easily arranged. Lord Melbourne showed me yesterday the *Declaration*, which is very simple and nice.

> Dearest Aunt [wrote the Prince that day to the Duchess of Kent],
> . . . You wish me to give you something I have worn. I send you the ring which you gave me at Kensington on Victoria's birthday in 1836. From that time it has never left my finger . . . . It has your name upon it, but the name is Victoria's too, and I beg you to wear it in remembrance of her and of myself. . . .

On 23 November the Privy Council were summoned to Buckingham Palace. The doors of the Bow Room were thrown open, recorded Mr Greville, and the Queen came in, 'attired in a plain morning gown, but wearing a bracelet containing Prince Albert's picture. She read the declaration in a clear, sonorous, sweet-toned voice, but her hands trembled so excessively that I wonder she was able to read the paper which she held.' After the Council was over, she hastened down to Windsor.

> Just arrived here, 5.30 [she told Prince Albert]. Everything has gone off very well. . . . The Council was held at two o'clock: more than a hundred persons were present, and *there* I had to read the Declaration. *It was rather an awful moment, to be obliged to announce this to so many people, many of whom were quite strangers, but they told me I did it very well, and I felt so happy to do it. . . .*
> *Everybody, they tell me, is very much pleased, and I wish you could have seen the crowds of people who cheered me loudly as I left the Palace for Windsor.* I am so happy today! Oh, if only *you* could be here!

The Queen, for all her nervousness, was utterly decided. From the first, she was overwhelmingly in love. But the nation was not, as she imagined, 'very much pleased'. They rejoiced in her marriage, but they felt small enthusiasm at the thought of this unknown young man. Those who consulted *Prince Albert. His Country and Kindred* discovered that Coburg and Gotha combined were the size of Dorset, and that their gross annual revenue was £128,330. Prince Albert of Saxe-Coburg and Gotha hardly seemed a match for the Queen of England.

King Leopold I of the Belgians, Queen Victoria's uncle. Reproduced by gracious permission of Her Majesty The Queen.

He comes, the bridegroom of Victoria's choice,
The nominee of Lehzen's vulgar voice;
He comes to take 'for better or for worse'
England's fat Queen and England's fatter purse. . . .
Saxe-Coburg sends him from its paltry race,
With foreign phrases and mustachio'd face,
To win from Hymen, and a school-girl's love,
Treasures, his sire's whole revenue above . . .
The hoyden Sovereign of this mighty isle
Welcomes her German with enraptured smile,
Telleth her 'faithful Commons' to provide
Supplies, to make him worthy of his bride;
And thus transforms, by magic conjuring,
A lucky beggar to a puissant king.

So wrote the author of *The German Bridegroom*. The feelings of the satirist were shared by Parliament. On 26 January, Mr Greville noted: 'Everybody . . . thinks the allowance proposed for Prince Albert very exorbitant: £50,000 a year given for pocket-money is quite monstrous, and it would have been prudent to propose a more moderate grant for the sake of his popularity.' Precedents were sought. Queen Anne, the last Queen Regnant, had married Prince George of Denmark ('very stupid and insignificant', wrote Victoria). Prince George, observed Mr Greville, had indeed enjoyed £50,000 a year, but his wife had given it to him. Parliament refused to vote £50,000 for Prince Albert; it reduced the sum to £30,000 a year. The Government motion was defeated by a majority of one hundred and four.

There was not only the problem of money. The Naturalization Bill provoked bad feeling in the House of Lords. King Leopold still interfered incessantly. He wanted Albert to be made a peer, because Prince George of Denmark (the Queen was growing weary of the name) had been created Duke of Kendal. King Leopold was wrong. Prince George had been created Duke of Cumberland. But in any case King Leopold's wishes were irrelevant. As the Queen observed, tartly: 'Dear Uncle is given to believe that he must rule the roast everywhere. However, that

is not a necessity.' The Queen did not want her future husband to be made a peer. Albert was not given a peerage.

Then there was the question of Albert's precedence. The Queen, wrote Mr Greville, 'is bent upon giving him precedence of the whole Royal Family. The Dukes of Sussex and Cambridge, who each want some additions to their incomes, have signified their consent; the King of Hanover (whom it does not immediately concern) has refused his.' He did not want to rank below 'a paper Royal Highness'. Again, Melbourne maintained that when an Heir Apparent to the throne was born, Albert could not take precedence of him. The Queen retorted that Albert's son could never precede his father. The Queen was accustomed to have her way. It was eventually settled that the Sovereign Will could grant Albert any precedence it wished.

Then the Tories behaved monstrously. When the Queen made her Declaration of Marriage, it was not specifically stated that Albert was a Protestant prince, and so perhaps – some said – he was Catholic. Baron Stockmar insisted that Albert belonged to the German Protestant Church, which in all points of faith and ritual was identical with the English; none the less, the Duke of Wellington moved and carried an amendment that the words 'Protestant Prince' be inserted in the Declaration. This was, observed the Queen, 'quite unnecessary, seeing that I *cannot* marry a *Papist*'. She said she would not invite the Duke of Wellington to her wedding.

Since she adored her future husband, she delighted to honour him; but, much as she adored him, she remained the Queen of England, and he had to be reminded of the fact. He thought, for instance, that he had the right to quarter the English Royal Arms with his own. 'As to the Arms,' wrote the Queen, '*as an English Prince you have no right, and Uncle Leopold had no right to quarter the English Arms, but the Sovereign has the power to allow it by Royal Command: this was done for Uncle Leopold by the Prince Regent, and I will do it again for you. But it can only be done by Royal Command.*'

A more important question was that of Prince Albert's Household. He had assumed that he would have a say in the matter. 'I should wish particularly that the selection should be made without regard to politics: for if I am really to keep myself free from all parties, my people must . . . be chosen from both sides – the same number of Whigs as Tories . . . I know you will agree.'

The Queen did not agree. 'As to your wish about your gentle-men, my dear Albert, I must tell you quite honestly that it will not do. You may entirely rely upon me that the people who will be about you will be absolutely pleasant people, of high standing and good character.' Again, he wanted a German as his private secretary. This time the Queen was rightly adamant. His private secretary must be English. In fact, she had already chosen him. Lord Melbourne, she wrote, 'has told me that young Mr Anson [his Private Secretary], who is with him, greatly wishes to be with you. I am very much in favour of it'. This choice, she said, would not look political, for Mr Anson had never been in Parliament (he was, in fact, a strong Whig, and he had been a Parliamentary candidate). However, Victoria was Queen, she knew what was right, and she chose all the Prince's Household before he had seen any of them. Again, he wrote to her, suggesting that the honeymoon at Windsor might be extended beyond the two or three days which she planned. 'But, dear Albert, you have not at all understood the matter. *You forget, my dearest Love, that I am the Sovereign, and that business can stop and wait for nothing. . . . Therefore two or three days is already a long time to be absent. . . . This is also my own wish in every way.*'

The moment for the marriage was now approaching. The Queen sent out an embassy to Gotha to invest her future husband with the Most Noble Order of the Garter. After due festivities, Duke Ernest and his sons set out for England. They travelled in the royal carriages which the Queen had lent for the occasion. She had decided that the wedding should not take place in Westminster Abbey, for that would be like another Coronation, but at the Chapel Royal, St James's. The fact that the building was smaller would also be convenient, for there would be little room for any of the detestable Tories. The Queen suggested that, as she would not drive to the wedding in full state, her mother should go with her in the carriage. The fact that she did not take that for granted shows how far apart mother and daughter had grown in the last three years.

On 6 February the Saxe-Coburgs sailed from Calais to Dover. They spent that night at the York Hotel, on the Esplanade. 'Dear beloved Victoria,' wrote the Prince next day,

. . . now I am in the same country as you. What a comforting thought for me! And to-morrow I shall be looking into your dear eyes. . . . We had a terrible crossing yesterday. . . . When we landed our faces were more the colour of wax candles than human visages. However, our reception was very satisfactory. . . .

The authorities are to come this morning with their Address, and I shall return thanks with the reply sent me from London. After that we set out for Canterbury. . . .

At Canterbury they were 'most heartily welcomed'. Next day, Saturday, 8 February, recorded the Queen's biographer, 'at half-past four in the pale light of a February afternoon, the travellers arrived at Buckingham Palace, and were received at the hall door by the Queen and the Duchess of Kent, attended by the whole household, to whom a worthy master had come.' No time was wasted. Half an hour later, the Prince took the oath of naturalization.

Next day, a Sunday, he and the Queen exchanged their wedding presents. She gave him the star and the badge of the Garter, and the Garter set in diamonds, and he gave her a sapphire and diamond brooch. They read over the marriage service together, 'and tried how to manage the *ring*'.

On Monday, 10 February, 'as if by a malignant influence', there were 'torrents of rain, and violent gusts of wind. Nevertheless a countless multitude thronged the park, and was scattered all over the town. I never beheld such a congregation as there was', wrote Mr Greville, 'in spite of the weather.' Not since the Allied Sovereigns visited London in 1814 had there been such a concourse of human beings. '*The Times* described the mass of spectators wedged in at the back of Carlton House Terrace and the foot of Constitution Hill, and the multitude of chairs, tables, benches, even casks, pressed into service, and affording vantage-ground to those who could pay for the accommodation. The dripping trees were also rendered available, and had their branches so laden with fruit, that brittle boughs gave way, while single specimens and small clusters of men and boys came rattling down on the heads and shoulders of confiding fellow-creatures.'

Dearest [wrote the Queen to Albert] – How are you today, and have you slept well? I have rested very well and feel very comfortable today. What weather! I believe, however, the rain will cease.

Send one word when you, my most dearly loved bridegroom, will be ready.

> Thy ever faithful,
> Victoria R.

Dear Grandmama [wrote Albert to the Duchess of Saxe-Gotha Altenburg],

In less than three hours I shall be standing before the altar with my dear bride. In that solemn moment I must once again ask for your blessing, which I am well assured I shall receive, and which shall be my protection and my joy. . . . May God be my helper!

The Queen drove in state from Buckingham Palace to St James's without any cheering, said Mr Greville, 'but then it was raining enough to damp warmer loyalty than that of a London mob. The procession in the Palace was pretty enough by all accounts.' The Duke of Wellington had, after all, been invited to the wedding. Prince Albert wore the uniform of a British Field-Marshal, and the Order of the Garter. He entered the Chapel Royal to the somewhat inappropriate tune of 'See, the Conquering Hero Comes!' The Queen wore a white satin wedding dress, with a deep flounce of Honiton lace, and a diamond necklace and earrings. Her uncle, the Duke of Sussex, gave her away. The Archbishop of Canterbury married her. He had enquired beforehand whether she wished to promise to obey her husband. Rather surprisingly, she did. 'She went through the ceremony', said Greville, 'with much grace and propriety, not without emotion'. After the service, a banquet was held at Buckingham Palace. The wedding cake, wrote her biographer,

> was three hundred pounds in weight, three yards [*sic*] in circumference, and fourteen inches in depth. In recognition of the national interest of the wedding, the figure of Hymen, on the top, was replaced by Britannia in the act of blessing the royal pair. . . . A Cupid wrote in a volume, spread open upon his knees, for the edification of the capering Cupids around, the auspicious '10th of February, 1840'.

After the reception, the Queen changed into a white silk dress trimmed with swansdown, and a white bonnet trimmed with a sprig of orange-blossom. Just before four o'clock she and her husband drove off to Windsor: 'I and Albert alone.'

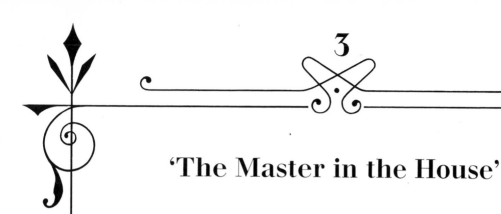

3

'The Master in the House'

'Really, I do not think it *possible* for anyone in the world to be *happier* or AS happy as I am. He is an Angel.' So the Queen wrote to her uncle next day, and from that opinion she never swerved. But she still remained the Queen of England. She allowed herself two days' honeymoon (which was, thought Mr Greville, 'more strange than delicate'); and then the whole Court followed her and her husband down to Windsor. They danced after dinner that night and the next; then back they went to London.

Some questions had been settled by marriage; others had not. On 25 February Mr Greville recorded: 'Besides the Precedence question, another is now raised about the Liturgy. The Queen wants to insert the Prince's name in it; they sent to me to know if Prince George's had been inserted, and I found it had not. . . . On looking into the Act of Uniformity, I satisfied myself that the Queen has not the power to insert his name.' As if this were not enough, there was the question of the Privy Council. The Prince would not be twenty-one until 26 August. In March the Lord Chancellor told Mr Greville that 'a difficulty had been started about making Prince Albert a Privy Councillor before he was of age'. Mr Greville consulted the Council books. He suggested, inevitably, that Prince Albert should be introduced on the same terms as Prince George of Denmark. Prince Albert was introduced on 11 September, when no one could deny that he was of age. He was so anxious to do his duty 'that, in the greater leisure of Windsor, he not only read Hallam's *Constitutional History* with the Queen, he began to read English law with a barrister'.

Stockmar was still beside him to remind him of his duty (for nearly two decades he was to live at Court for six months a year);

but almost at once the influence of Stockmar began to fade. He remained a consultant, but, if the Prince talked to anyone, he talked to his young Private Secretary. George Anson had been imposed on him; but almost from the beginning he became his intimate friend. Anson, said the Prince, was almost like a brother to him. The affection and respect were mutual. 'In no Person', wrote George Anson, had he seen 'so spotless and so pure a character as the Prince's'. Not until George Anson died in 1849 did Stockmar regain his position as confidential adviser.

The marriage had necessitated certain domestic changes. Until now, the Duchess of Kent had been living at Buckingham Palace, and she had had her apartment at Windsor, but these were now wanted for the Prince, and within a month the Duchess was gone. The Queen took Ingestre House in Belgrave Square for her mother, until, in the autumn, Clarence House became vacant. Albert was very fond of Aunt Kent, and he was distressed by the long estrangement between her and Victoria. He set to work to bring them together. He was tactful – but quite as determined – in his attitude to Baroness Lehzen. He did not hasten to get rid of her. The Queen was much attached to her. Lehzen had supported her in her unhappy childhood. But Lehzen could not see the difference which the Queen's marriage had made to her own position. She clung to a control that she should have relinquished. She interfered in matters that did not concern her. Albert quietly set out to make himself essential. That was the surest way to make Lehzen unnecessary.

Baroness Lehzen. Miniature by Koepke. Copyright reserved.

It was true that Albert did not understand the English; but – which was most important – he understood the Queen. She tried to please him in everything, and almost at once his influence began to be felt. Victoria had been furious when the Tories cut his annuity, and she had sworn that she would not ask Wellington to her wedding. However, she had repented, and asked him. She also invited him to one of her first dinner-parties, and Albert was extremely attentive to him. Victoria had decided that she would have no more to do with Sir Robert Peel; Albert made friends with him. There was a general feeling of conciliation.

There was also intense private happiness. On 15 March Lady Palmerston (the former Lady Cowper) reported:

The Queen and P. Albert are very happy in their marriage . . . He is

very good looking and amiable and charming, and pleases every body that approaches him. Even the mob, who are much taken with his looks and agreeable expression, so that I hope they will now become quite popular! The Queen has a dinner and Dance afterwards, every Monday.

Miss Liddell, the future Lady Bloomfield, a Maid of Honour, remembered: 'One lovely summer's morning we had danced till dawn, and the quadrangle being then open to the east, Her

Majesty went out on the roof of the portico to see the sun rise. . . .
It rose behind St Paul's, which we saw quite distinctly; Westminster Abbey and the trees in the Green Park stood out against a golden sky.'

Prince Albert was determined to work for the good of the nation. He therefore had to acquire political influence. He meant to make himself the Queen's sole counsellor: to put his will, his ability so much at her service that they became her own. But he had to be cautious. As she had warned him, the English would strongly resent any interference from him in politics. She herself was jealous – and rightly so – of her sovereignty. She and her Ministers, and they alone, were directors of the realm. But she appreciated her husband's noble nature. She felt protective towards the man who had left everything for her sake. A fortnight after the marriage, his father had returned to Coburg. Albert was desolate. His brother stayed on till May, and their parting brought him anguish. When Ernest had gone, he could only say: 'Such things are hard to bear.' 'Oh!' wrote the Queen in her journal, 'How I did feel for my dearest precious husband at this moment! Father, brother, friends, country – all he has left, and all for me. God grant I may be the happy person, the *most* happy person, to make this dearest, blessed being happy and contented. What is in my power to make him happy, I will do.' The Prince was far from happy. 'I am only the husband,' he wrote, 'not the master in the house.'

He recognized that this was a moment to advance a step. The Queen knew that he was lonely, and he reproached her for not taking him into her confidence. She consulted Melbourne. Melbourne was anxious 'that the Queen should tell and shew [her husband] everything connected with public affairs'. She took his advice, and, before the marriage was six months old, Melbourne was sending Prince Albert Foreign Office despatches. Occasionally, at the Queen's invitation, the Prince attended her audiences with her Ministers.

Prince Albert had been naturalized. He wanted a central place in English politics. But he remained – as he recognized – 'a true Coburger' at heart. He was shy and ill at ease, and he behaved with frigid dignity. His tastes showed no trace of anglicization.

He thought of all sports as diversions; he could not understand why the English were so serious about them. He admired pursuits which the English dismissed as drawing-room accomplishments. With his feminine tastes, his lack of humour, his wholly un-English traits, he was not likely to be popular. Yet those few people who knew him admired his invaluable qualities. His good sense was already doing much to conciliate resentment at the Queen's high-handed behaviour in politics. 'The Tories are very friendly to me', he wrote, 'as I am also to them.'

The Prince had also reconciled the Queen and her mother, and their reconciliation warmed into love. He was a peacemaker, and he soothed his wife's impulsive and sometimes violent temper. His seriousness of purpose, his industry, his respectability were exactly what was wanted to obliterate the Hanoverian past. He made his first public speech at an Anti-Slave Trade meeting. He was still so uncertain of English that he learned his speech by heart and rehearsed it with the Queen. But it was, he assured his father, 'received with great applause, and seems to have produced a good effect in the country. This rewards me sufficiently for the fear and nervousness I had to conquer'.

In June, by chance, there was a sudden occasion for loyalty. He and the Queen were driving one evening up Constitution Hill, to call on the Duchess of Kent. A crazy young man, Edward Oxford, fired two pistol shots at them at a range of five or six yards. Even Mr Greville praised the Queen's behaviour. She showed, he considered, 'perfect courage and self-possession, and exceeding propriety'. She and her husband drove on to the Duchess's house in Belgrave Square, and then they continued their drive in the park, to show the public, as Albert wrote, 'that we had not, on account of what had happened, lost all confidence in them'. Nothing could have been more popular than such simple courage; and presumably the incident was remembered when, the following month, the Regency Bill came before Parliament. The Queen was expecting her first baby in November ('I was in for it at once', she recalled, 'and furious I was'). The Bill provided that, should she die in childbirth, like Princess Charlotte, or before the heir to the throne came of age, the Prince should be appointed Regent without a controlling Council. He would thus, until the yet unborn child reached the age of eighteen, be to all intents and purposes King of England. When the Queen was due to prorogue Parliament, the question arose of where the Prince should sit. 'We must see', muttered Melbourne, 'what happened to that infernal George of Denmark'. Parliament was prorogued in August. Albert sat next to the throne, to which – should there be a catastrophe – he would practically succeed.

The Queen gave birth to her first child on 21 November. 'Oh, madam!' said the doctor, 'it is a Princess'. 'Well,' said the Queen, 'next time it will be a Prince.'

The Court went to Windsor for Christmas 1840. It was now with great reluctance that the Queen returned to town at the end of January. The reason was evident: Prince Albert hated late hours and London fogs; he liked to escape to the hill above the Thames. 'I told Albert', wrote the Queen in her journal, 'that formerly I was too happy to go to London, and wretched to leave it, and now since the blessed hour of our marriage, I like and am unhappy to leave the country and could be content and happy never to go to town. . . . The solid pleasures of a peaceful, quiet yet merry life in the country, with my inestimable husband and friend, my all in all, are far more durable than the amusements of London.'

In London, as far as possible, they continued their peaceful, quiet yet merry existence. They breakfasted every morning at nine, and then – perhaps with Eos, the Prince's greyhound – they took a walk in the gardens of Buckingham Palace. Some of these fifty acres had once been the Mulberry Gardens of James I. The Prince, we are told, 'enlivened the gardens with different kinds of animals and aquatic birds, a modified version of the *Thier-Garten* so often found in connection with royal residences in Germany.' He taught the birds to come when he whistled to them. After the morning walk came official business; and then – at least in the early years of their marriage – the Queen and her husband drew and etched together. Luncheon followed at two o'clock. In the afternoon, Lord Melbourne had an audience of the Queen, and between five and six Prince Albert usually drove her out in a phaeton. Dinner was at eight o'clock. In the evening the Prince played double chess. He read aloud most days to his wife.

He showed a German love of music. He was happiest when he

Windsor Castle from a Victorian photograph.
Reproduced by gracious permission of Her Majesty The Queen.

was improvising on his new organ at Buckingham Palace. He encouraged the Queen in her singing, and he himself sang with her. Indeed, they gave a concert, and sang 'Non funeste crudele' by Ricci, and the Queen sang 'Dunque il mio bene' from Mozart's *Magic Flute* with Rubini and Lablache, the most prestigious tenor and bass of the Italian opera. When there was not music, the Prince would have liked to invite scientists and literary men to the Palace, but King Leopold had warned the Queen against the society of artistic people; and besides, as Lord Melbourne understood, she did not like to think that she could not share in their conversation.

Sometimes, however, the world of art burst in upon them. In May 1841 an actress of genius arrived from Paris. Rachel was a pedlar's daughter, and the unquestioned star of the Comédie-Française. She had resurrected French classical tragedy. Now she arrived to conquer the London public. Late in May, she announced to a friend: 'On Wednesday I am to appear before the Queen at Marlborough House. The whole Court will be there! I am very frightened!'

An awe-inspiring occasion it was for so young a girl. 'Her Majesty the Queen Dowager had yesterday an evening party at her residence, Marlborough House, Pall Mall', recorded the Court Circular on 3 June. 'Mademoiselle Rachel attended during the evening.' There, for the first time, Rachel performed before Queen Victoria. They faced each other, the girl of twenty who, knowing nothing of civilization, had brought a dead art to life; and the girl of twenty-two who was 'so to dominate the entire earth that she seemed a chief and permanent part of modern civilization'. Rachel recited mostly from *Cinna*, and the Queen, though she thought French tragedy 'always formal and stilted', decided that 'Mlle Rachel is perfect, in her diction and interpretation'. When, next morning, Lady Normanby arrived with an invitation from the Queen: 'Can you imagine,' asked Rachel, 'all my delight and happiness?' Her triumph was complete. The following day Her Majesty went with Prince Albert to see '*Horace* with the 5th act left out', and 'we were', she wrote in her journal, 'delighted with Mlle Rachel, whose acting was perfect. She was completely draped in white, and her little countenance looked so well. She was so simple, natural and unaffected, full of intense feeling, both of grief and great anger, and very dignified.'

Queen Victoria could not disguise admiration any more than dislike; before the month was out, the King of the Belgians had been informed, without reticence, of her pleasure and her invitation:' We are, and so is *everybody here*, so charmed with Mme Rachel; she is perfect, *et puis*, such a nice modest girl; she is going to declaim at Windsor.'

On 10 June, an anxious Rachel arrived by train ('most comfortable') at Windsor. The company who had gathered at Marlborough House paled in comparison with the 'very numerous party' who had spent the day at Ascot and had now returned to a banquet in St George's Hall. While they were busy dining, a royal carriage was sent for Rachel. She recited that evening, in the Green Drawing-Room, to an audience of three hundred, including several dukes, lesser peers by the score, and, no less significant, Baroness Lehzen,'whose appearance was that of a very soberly dressed parrot'. The Queen decided: 'She recited and acted quite beautifully . . . I talked to Mlle Rachel, after her last performance. She really is *most* pleasing. The Ds of Sutherland then went behind the curtain, where she was sitting, and gave her from me a blue enamel and diamond bracelet.' 'A very pretty bracelet', the recipient wrote home, 'and I had supper at Windsor Castle, after the most gracious and flattering reception'. Before the season was over, the Queen went twice to see Rachel at Her Majesty's Theatre, and threw her roses on the stage out of her own bouquet.

At Buckingham Palace and at Windsor there was domestic felicity.

> I hated the thought of having children [the Queen was one day to tell her eldest daughter], and have no adoration for very little babies, . . . still I know what a fuss and piece of work was made with you; far too much I think, for it was not good to dress you as often as you were, and to have you up so late. I used to have you in my dressing room – while I dressed for dinner, dancing on Mrs Pegley's [the nurse's] knee – till you got so lively that you could not sleep at night. All that was very foolish, and I warn you against it – but one is very foolish with one's first child.

Political life was less delightful. In this summer of 1841 the Whig Government seemed about to fall. On 4 June a vote of 'No confidence' in the Administration was defeated by only one vote. On 14 June Prince Albert went to Oxford, where he was made a Doctor of Civil Law. He was well received, but the Queen's Ministers, 'individually and collectively, were hissed and hooted with all the vehemence of Oxonian Toryism. Her Majesty', noted Mr Greville, 'must learn to bear with such manifestations of sentiment.' Perhaps it was now that the Queen took a violent dislike to Oxford – 'that old monkish place, which I have a horror of'. Certainly she did not approve of Mr Greville's outspokenness. Years later, when his *Memoirs* were published, she was enraged by his 'indiscretion, indelicacy, ingratitude towards friends, betrayal of confidence, and shameful disloyalty towards his Sovereign'.

Meanwhile, in the summer of 1841, Victoria and Albert made a stately progress round the homes of the nobility. They stayed with the Duke of Bedford at Woburn Abbey. On leaving Woburn, so the Queen reported, 'a crowd of good, loyal people rode with us part of the way. They so pressed and pushed that it was as if we were out hunting'. They went on to Panshanger, Earl Cowper's, and Brocket Hall, Lord Melbourne's, returning by Hatfield, the Marquess of Salisbury's. On 1 August they returned to Windsor. Next day the Prince told his father: 'We are highly delighted with the beautiful things we have seen, and the heartiness and enthusiasm of the reception we have everywhere received. There genuinely is still in the English country-people an extraordinary amount of religious feeling and devotion to the Throne, the law and the Church, which it is most gratifying to see.'

The first tokens of official acceptance were being bestowed upon the Prince. No doubt the Oxford doctorate gratified the earnest intellectual who had barely passed his student days. But the Prince who was thus honoured by the English Establishment still remained out of tune with English feeling. His degree had been conferred on the eve of the anniversary of Waterloo; and the Duke of Wellington – Chancellor of Oxford University – had invited him to his Waterloo Dinner. The Prince, recorded Mr Greville, 'sent an excuse, which was a mistake, for the invitation was a great compliment, and this is a sort of national commemoration at which he might have felt a pride at being present.'

Albert made unhappy errors of judgment; he remained an

Daguerreotype of Prince Albert taken at Brighton, 6 March 1842. It is the earliest photograph of the Prince. Reproduced by gracious permission of Her Majesty The Queen.

incorrigible foreigner. But he was already showing his political mastery. In August the Whigs resigned, and the Queen asked Sir Robert Peel to form a government. It was bitter to lose Lord Melbourne; for more than four years she had seen him almost daily. But in his last audience he had praised Prince Albert's judgment and discretion. Since he himself was leaving her, she could not – he said – do better than seek the Prince's advice on all political matters, and confidently rely on his judgment. She did so. In September she and Albert went to Claremont for a few days' quiet; and there she held the Council at which the new Ministers were appointed. She had once shown her resentment of Peel; now she charmed him by her composure and her dignity. Mr Gladstone held the first office of his political career, that of Vice-President of the Board of Trade. He told the Prince's secretary, Anson: 'There was not one of the new government who did not place the fullest confidence in Her Majesty's intended fairness towards them.' There were other signs that the Queen was influenced by her husband's judgment. The change of Government brought changes in the Royal Household. Mr Greville discussed the appointments with the Duke of Wellington; and the Duke confirmed that it was the Prince who had insisted upon spotless character.

The Prince's good relations with Peel were already beginning to bear fruit. Soon after he came to office, Sir Robert suggested that there should be a Royal Commission to encourage the fine arts in the United Kingdom. He asked the Prince if he would preside. It was a presidency after Albert's heart.

'If an art spirit has been born amongst us and is being cultivated, the change is mainly due to the exertion and influence of the Prince Consort.' So wrote the author of *England's Royal Home*, some years after Prince Albert had died. The statement was sweeping, but it was true that he had done much to foster art. In 1851, when he attended the Royal Academy dinner, he could say that, since his arrival in England, he had never missed a Royal Academy Exhibition; he spoke of the harm that could be done by harsh criticism, and urged the need of kindness in judging art. Early in his married life, he had won the respect of English artists. He visited their studios, and showed his appreciation of their work. When Frith exhibited *Derby Day* at the Royal

Academy, he was astonished by the Prince's knowledge 'of what I may call the *conduct* of a picture . . . I put many of the Prince's suggestions to the proof,' so he remembered, 'after the close of the Exhibition, and I improved my picture in every instance'. The Prince was a frequent visitor to the studio of John Martin. He warmly admired his Romantic, apocalyptic work, and he commissioned a painting, *The Eve of the Deluge*, which now hangs in Buckingham Palace.

Prince Albert's 'greatest amusement and delight', said the Queen, was the print-room of the Royal Library. He found the drawings in disorder, and decided that they should be properly arranged. He broke up the albums of Raphael drawings, and mounted them on sunk mounts to preserve them better. He collected engravings and photographs of every known fragment of Raphael's work. He was a pioneer in the use of photography for comparative studies. As for the paintings in the royal collection, he found that hundreds of them were stacked in the cellars at Hampton Court, and he arranged for them to be cleaned and hung. He also enlarged the collection himself. At a time when the National Gallery contained no Italian pictures of the fourteenth century, only two of the fifteenth century, and only one early Flemish picture, Prince Albert bought early paintings with discrimination.

He also helped to rouse Government interest in the arts. He found the politicians dilatory where artistic matters were concerned, and he made it his business to lay such matters before the Cabinet. He was partly responsible for the erection of Cleopatra's Needle. He saw that eventually the state would have to replace the private patron. He constantly urged that people should have more facilities for seeing pictures, and that the public galleries should be made more attractive. In 1848 he arranged for an important collection of early Italian paintings to be exhibited at Kensington Palace. When he owner fell into financial troubles, the Prince himself acquired them. In accordance with his wishes, twenty-two of them were given to the National Gallery on his death.

At forty-eight minutes past ten on the morning of Tuesday, 9 November 1841, the Queen fulfilled the promise which she had made on the birth of the Princess Royal. She was delivered of the hoped-for son. *God Save the Queen* was heartily sung in all the theatres, and 'great joy manifested generally. The event', as Mr. Greville remarked, 'came very opportunely for the Lord Mayor's dinner.'

Yet even the birth of the Prince of Wales – like much in the early days of the marriage – created unexpected complications. It had, some said, been the custom for the officer on guard at St James's Palace to be promoted major when a royal child was born. However, the guard had been relieved at forty-five minutes past ten that morning, when the new guard marched into Palace Yard; and the Prince of Wales was born three minutes later. The guard was therefore in the actual process of being changed. Which officer was entitled to promotion? Heads were bent over the records, and it was discovered that no precedent existed after all; but such was the general goodwill that the captain of the old guard was none the less accorded a majority.

During the Queen's confinement 'all the boxes and business' had been sent as usual to the Palace, and the boxes had been opened and returned by the Prince. He had established this practice the previous year. But while he was more and more concerned with affairs of state, and took an increasing part in English politics, he still refused to forget his German birth. On 5 December, before the Prince of Wales was a month old, Mr Greville wrote indignantly: 'The Queen and Prince are very anxious to allot to this baby his armorial bearings, and they wish that he should quarter the arms of Saxony with the royal arms of England, because Prince Albert is alleged to be *Duke of Saxony. . . .*' On 9 December: 'They have gazetted the child "Duke of Saxony", which is very absurd, and at Lady Holland's, last night, the precedence given to that title over the English titles was much criticized.' As if this was not enough, the King of Prussia was invited to be godfather to the heir to the throne. In January he arrived for the christening, and he landed at Greenwich to be met by the Duke of Wellington in the uniform of a Prussian field-marshal.

On 10 February, two years to the day after the Queen's marriage, Lord Melbourne told Mr Greville that her Ministers seemed 'to pay great court to the Prince, whom the Queen delights to honour and to elevate, and . . . he would probably acquire greater influence every day'. Lord Melbourne's pro-

The christening of the Prince of Wales at St George's Chapel, Windsor Castle, 25 January 1842. The chief sponsor was King Frederick William IV of Prussia (fifth from the left, in group with the Duke and Duchess of Cambridge, and the Duchess of Kent). Behind the Queen and Prince Albert is the Duke of Wellington with the Sword of State, and on Prince Albert's left, the Duke of Sussex. Painting by Sir George Hayter. Copyright reserved.

phecy was to be fulfilled. Yet, almost as he made it, the Queen displayed her own surpassing royalty. This month, she opened Parliament. She looked

> worthy and fit [thought Mme Bunsen, the wife of the Prussian Minister], to be the converging-point of so many rays of grandeur. It is self-evident that she is not tall, but were she ever so tall, she could not have more grace and dignity. . . . In short it could not be said that she *did well*, but that she was *the Queen* – she was, and felt herself to be, the descendant of her ancestors.

The old political order was changing, but the Queen was not forgetful of the past. Early this year the future Bishop Wilberforce visited Windsor. Melbourne, too, was a visitor, and 'the Queen's meeting with him was very interesting. The exceeding pleasure which lighted up her countenance was', said Wilberforce, 'quite touching. His behaviour to her was perfect – the fullest attentive deference of the subject with a subdued air of "your father's friend" that was quite fascinating.'

The Queen had been feeling low after the birth of the Prince of Wales, and the family of four went to stay at the Royal Pavilion at Brighton. The palace exuded the charm and taste and fantasy of 'dear Uncle King'. The Queen disliked Brighton, and thought the Pavilion 'a strange, odd Chinese looking thing'. One can imagine the Prince's distaste for this entrancing extravaganza. He had no humour, no elegance, no exuberant imagination. The thought of the Hanoverians alarmed him. He never liked the Pavilion, and he found no privacy there. He and the Queen did not go there after 1845. The stripping of the Pavilion began in 1846, and, during the next two years, one hundred and forty-three vanloads of furniture, decorations, porcelain, clocks and carpets were removed to the other royal palaces.

In 1847 a sale of furniture and *objets d'art* was held; in 1848 the remaining items were sold and disposed of, the doors were locked, and the keys were sent to the Lord Chamberlain. However, opposition arose to the Government's proposal to acquire and demolish the Pavilion. A loan of £60,000 was arranged with the Bank of England, and in 1850 – to the lasting pleasure of posterity – the Royal Pavilion Estate became the property of the town of Brighton.

Meanwhile, in 1842, the Royal Family of four returned from Brighton to London, and in May the Queen gave a fancy-dress ball at which she and her husband appeared as Edward III and Queen Philippa. It was the first of a series of royal costume balls which were to delight Society.

There were more serious moments. The summer of 1842 brought a visitor of particular distinction. Felix Mendelssohn arrived in London. On 13 June, at a Philharmonic Society concert, he conducted his A minor Symphony for the first time. On 20 June he was summoned to Buckingham Palace.

He himself described the occasion.

> Queen Victoria [he told his mother] is pretty and most charming; she looks very youthful, and she is gentle, courteous and gracious. She speaks good German and knows all my music well. Yesterday evening I was sent for by the Queen, who was almost alone with Prince Albert, and she seated herself near the piano and made me play to her; first seven of the *Songs without Words*, then the *Serenade*, two impromptus on *Rule Britannia*, Lutzow's *Wilde Jagd* and *Gaudeamus Igitur*. The latter was somewhat difficult, but remonstrance was out of the question, and as they gave the themes, of course it was my duty to play them. Then I saw the splendid grand gallery in Buckingham Palace where they drank tea, and where two wild boars by Paul Potter are hanging, and a good many other pictures which pleased me well. . . .

Before he left England, Mendelssohn paid a second visit to the Palace; it was even more remarkable than the first. As he wrote home:

> Prince Albert had asked me to go to him on Saturday, at 2 o'clock, so that I might try his organ before I left England; I found him alone, and as we were talking the Queen came in, also alone, in a simple morning dress. She said she was obliged to leave for Claremont in an hour. . . .
>
> I begged that the Prince would first play me something; and he played a Chorale, by heart, with the pedals, so charmingly, and clearly, and correctly, that it would have done credit to any professional. Then it was my turn, and I began my chorus from *St Paul* – 'How lovely are the messengers'. Before I got to the end of the first verse they both joined in the chorus, and all the time Prince Albert managed the stops for me so cleverly that I was really quite en-

chanted. Then the Queen asked if I had written any new songs, and said she was very fond of singing my published ones. 'You should sing one to him', said Prince Albert; . . . and she sang the Pilgerspruch 'Lass dich nur', really quite faultlessly, and with charming feeling and expression. And then Prince Albert said I must play him something, and, just as if I was to keep nothing but the pleasantest, most charming recollection of it, I never improvised better; and they followed me with so much intelligence and attention that I felt more at my ease than I ever did in improvising to an audience. The Queen said several times she hoped I would soon come to England again and pay them a visit, and then I took leave; and down below I saw the beautiful carriages waiting, with their scarlet outriders, and in a quarter of an hour the flag was lowered, and the Court Circular announced: 'Her Majesty left the Palace at 20 minutes past three.'

Prince Albert had given Mendelssohn a ring engraved 'V.R. 1842'; and Mendelssohn was to dedicate his Scottish Symphony to Queen Victoria.

Of all modern composers, Mendelssohn was the Prince's favourite; and, when he returned to London in 1844, the Prince went to hear him conduct a performance of *St Paul*. The following year, when he again conducted the oratorio in London, the Queen and her husband were both present. In April 1847 he visited England for the last time. He conducted *Elijah* in Exeter Hall. The Queen and Prince Albert both attended; and the Prince inscribed his own copy of the work 'to the Noble Artist who, surrounded by the Baal-worship of debased art, has been able by his genius and science, like another Elijah, faithfully to preserve the worship of true art.'

This was the climax of Mendelssohn's visit to England; indeed it was almost the climax of his life. He died on 4 November, at the age of thirty-eight. Prince Albert's biographer maintains that the Prince's appreciation of his work 'gave an unmistakable stimulus to the highest branch of composition – the Oratorio – in this country'. A selection from Mendelssohn's *St Paul* was given on 28 June 1861, in the last concert which the Prince arranged.

Music was Prince Albert's favourite art, it was the one which gave him most refreshment and delight. He was an accomplished singer and player, and he had a passion for organ music. He himself composed a *Jubilate* and a *Sanctus*, and his chorale 'In

Life's gay morn' was sung by Jenny Lind at the marriage of the Prince of Wales. His *Te Deum* in C was sung by a choir of three hundred at the Queen's Golden Jubilee Service in Westminster Abbey in 1887.

Prince Albert reorganized the Queen's private band, and changed it from wind to strings. He arranged the programmes for the state and semi-state occasions on which the band performed. He did much to form musical taste in England, and to prepare for the rebirth of English music in the later years of the Queen's reign. In the middle years of the nineteenth century, the two main organizations for concerts were the Philharmonic Society and the Ancient Concerts. During the 1840s the Prince was often Director of the Ancient Concerts, and he selected the music. Sir Theodore Martin, his official biographer, records that, under his auspices, Schubert's *Fierabras* overture, Mendelssohn's *Athalie*, and Schumann's B Flat Symphony received their first performances in England. In 1855 the Prince arranged for Wagner to conduct the overture to *Tannhauser*.

On 29 August 1842 Victoria and Albert set out on their first visit to Scotland. 'At 5 o'clock in the morning', the Queen recorded, 'we left Windsor by the railroad. . . . We reached London at a quarter to six and arrived at Woolwich before seven. Albert and I immediately stepped into our barge. There was a large crowd to see us embark.' The Queen's yacht, *The Royal George*, was commanded by Lord Adolphus FitzClarence, one of the natural sons of William IV. In some ways no one was less Victorian than the Queen herself. She was perfectly prepared to accept an illegitimate cousin at Court; and Adolphus FitzClarence assured Mr Greville that

> . . . nothing could be more agreeable and amiable than she was, and the Prince, too, on board the yacht, conversing all the time with perfect ease and good humour, and on all subjects, taking great interest and very curious about everything in the ship, dining on deck in the midst of the sailors, making them dance, talking to the boatswain, and, in short, doing everything that was popular and ingratiating. Her chief fault, in little things and in great, seems to be impatience; in sea phrase, she always wants to *go ahead*; she can't bear contradiction nor to be thwarted. She was put out because she could

The Royal George off Inchkeith, in sight of Edinburgh, 1 September 1842. Watercolour by J. W. Carmichael. Reproduced by gracious permission of Her Majesty The Queen.

not get quicker to the end of her voyage, and land so soon as she wished. She insisted on landing as soon as it was possible, and would not wait till the authorities were ready and the people assembled to receive her. . . .

The Queen gave her own version of events.

Thursday, September 1.

At a quarter to one o'clock, we heard the anchor let down – a welcome sound. At seven we went on deck, where we breakfasted. Close on one side were Leith and the high hills towering over Edinburgh, which was in fog; and on the other side was to be seen the Isle of May (where it was said Macduff held out against Macbeth), the Bass Rock being behind us. At ten minutes past eight we arrived at Granton Pier, where we were met by the Duke of Buccleuch, Sir Robert Peel and others. We then stepped over a gangway on to the pier, the people cheering, and the Duke saying that he begged to be allowed to welcome us.

The impression Edinburgh has made upon us is very great; it is quite beautiful, totally unlike anything else I have ever seen; and what is even more, Albert, who has seen so much, says it is unlike anything *he* ever saw. The enthusiasm was very great, and the people were very friendly and kind.

She and her husband spent the night at Dalkeith, in the house of the Duke of Buccleuch; and there, next morning – despite her unfortunate tendency to plumpness – she revelled in porridge and finnan haddock for breakfast. She and the Prince continued to sing the praises of Edinburgh.

The view of Edinburgh from the road before you enter Leith is [declared the Queen] quite enchanting; it is, as Albert said, fairy-like, and what you would only imagine as a thing to dream of, or to see in a picture. There was that beautiful large town hall, all of stone (no mingled colours of brick to mar it), with the bold castle on one side, and the Calton Hill on the other, with those high sharp hills of Arthur's Seat and Salisbury Crags towering above all, and making the finest, boldest background imaginable. Albert said he felt sure the Acropolis could not be finer.

The royal couple were not only swept off their feet by Edinburgh; the Queen was struck by the handsomeness of the kilted Highland soldiers, by the lilt of bagpipes and the intricacies of the sword-dance. At Lord Breadalbane's castle, Taymouth, 'the firing of the guns, the cheering of the great crowd, the picturesqueness of the dresses, the beauty of the surrounding country, with its rich background of wooded hills, altogether formed one of the finest scenes imaginable'. 'It seemed', she wrote, 'as if a great chieftain in olden feudal times was receiving his sovereign. It was princely and romantic. . . . After dinner the grounds were most splendidly illuminated – a whole chain of lamps along the railings, and on the ground was written in lamps, "Welcome Victoria–Albert". There were some pretty fireworks, and the whole ended by the Highlanders dancing reels which they do to perfection, to the sound of the pipes, by torchlight, in front of the house. It had a wild and very gay effect.' Next day the Prince went shooting, and bagged nineteen roe-deer, several hares and pheasants, and three brace of grouse. The Queen was rowed up Loch Tay, and the boatmen sang Gaelic boat-songs which she found 'very wild and singular'. On 14 September she lamented in her journal: 'This is our last day in Scotland; it is really a delightful country, and I am very sorry to leave it.'

Lord Aberdeen was instructed to write to the Lord Advocate: 'The Queen will leave Scotland with a feeling of regret that her visit on this occasion could not be further prolonged. . . . The devotion and enthusiasm evinced in every quarter, and by all ranks, have produced an impression on the mind of Her Majesty which can never be effaced.' Seldom was an official assurance to be more amply justified.

On their return south, the Queen and her husband travelled to Windsor. Lady Lyttelton, who had been a lady-in-waiting since the Queen's accession, was now in command of the royal nurseries. There could hardly have been a happier choice. Lady Lyttelton was the former Lady Sarah Spencer, elder daughter of the second Earl Spencer. She was fifty-five, motherly, charming, strict and understanding. She was to keep her responsible post until 1851, when she retired at the age of sixty-three.

There are engaging pictures of the royal nursery in the early years of the marriage. We catch a glimpse of the Princess Royal, in dark blue velvet and white shoes, and yellow kid gloves, displaying her new dresses, and bidding Miss Liddell – a lady-in-waiting – try one of them on. The Princess Royal – reported Stockmar – was as round as a little barrel. She was vivacious, intelligent, and already alive to her dignity. The Queen herself was corrected when she ventured to call her 'Missy', and Lady Lyttelton was warned off in kindergarten French: 'N'approchez-pas moi, moi ne veux pas vous.'

The Princess Royal, known as Pussy, was a delight from birth. The Prince of Wales was, it seems, a problem child. On their return from Scotland in this autumn of 1842, his parents found him sadly backward for a child of ten months. However, Prince Albert and Stockmar were already planning his education. Education, wrote the Prince, 'is the preparation for the future life. . . .' Education, said Stockmar, began at birth.

Queen Victoria disliked maternity. Though she became the mother of nine children, she found pregnancy and childbirth a vexing obligation of marriage. When, in time, her eldest daughter was happily pregnant, the Queen wrote: 'I know your rather too great passion for very little babies, and I wish to guard you against overdoing the thing, . . . so that you should forget your duties to your husband, your station and indeed your relations.' The Queen felt profound affection for her family, and there are abundant verbal pictures of Victoria and her growing flock of children. But while her husband was alive, he meant incomparably more to her than any son or daughter could ever do. 'All the numerous children', she told her uncle, 'are as nothing to me when he is away. It seems as if the whole life of the house and the home were gone.'

The Prince was, in general, kind to his children. He danced a country-dance with them to usher in the New Year. He swung the smallest of them between his legs in a large table-napkin. He gave a pop-gun to his youngest son, who took a pot-shot at him, and then, to make amends, presented arms. He adored the Princess Royal; and, when she married, she told the Queen: 'I think it will kill me to take leave of dear Papa'. He also felt particularly fond of his second daughter, Princess Alice. She based her whole life on what she imagined he would have wished, and her dying words were to be 'dear Papa'. Lady Augusta Bruce (sometime lady-in-waiting) considered that 'the beloved parents have nothing so much at heart as the right training of these precious children'.

It is sad that they both failed, lamentably, to understand their eldest son. 'I wish', wrote the Queen, 'that he should grow up entirely under *his Father's eye*, and every step be guided by him, so that when he has attained the age of sixteen or seventeen he may be a real companion to his father.' It was a curious ambition. She wanted her son, in fact, to be a replica of her husband. Neither of them considered that he might be born with a different nature. They did not, for a moment, study the character of the Prince of Wales. They imposed their theories upon him.

There is no doubt that they did so with excellent intentions. They both felt that the proper training of the heir to the throne was their duty to the country, and their apprehensions were evident. When the Prince of Wales was born, his father had said that 'the greatest object must be to make him as unlike as possible to any of his [Hanoverian] great-uncles'. How could this likeness be avoided? Stockmar was consulted. He explained that the weaknesses of George IV had been due to a faulty education. The Prince of Wales must therefore be given an education that was 'truly moral and truly English'. The Coburg Prince took the advice of the Coburg Baron.

Instinct and appreciation played no part in the upbringing of the Prince of Wales. His innate good qualities were not recognized or encouraged; his shortcomings were ruthlessly corrected. Lady Lyttelton saw that he was not clever; but she also saw that he was truthful and possessed of 'very good principles'. The fact that he had good principles was, apparently, dismissed. The fact that he was not clever was something which the Queen and her husband felt morally obliged to remedy. Bertie was warm, impulsive and affectionate ('the Pr. of Wales', wrote Lady Augusta Bruce, 'is full of love and attention'). Bertie had natural charm; he was a Hanoverian, like his mother. The Queen was determined that Bertie should be exactly like his father: moral, reserved and intellectual. 'I wish you were one and all [Papa's] image', she wrote to her eldest daughter. 'Alas! Some are not!'

In time Lady Lyttelton gave up her charge – and not, alas, to the tutor suggested by Baron Bunsen, the Prussian Minister. Arthur Stanley, the future Dean of Westminster (and future husband of Lady Augusta Bruce), would have been an excellent mentor. Instead, the Queen and the Prince appointed the Reverend Henry Birch,

Group, April 1857. L. to R.: Colonel (later Sir) Charles Phipps (one of Prince Albert's private secretaries), F. W. Gibbs (tutor to the Prince of Wales), the Prince of Wales, Prince Albert, Baron Stockmar, Dr Becker (librarian to Prince Albert, and tutor), Baron Ernst Stockmar (son of Baron Stockmar). Photograph by Caldesi. Reproduced by gracious permission of Her Majesty The Queen.

Group, December 1858: the Prince of Wales and others, including Colonel Bruce (left) and the Rev. A. P. Stanley (2nd left). Reproduced by gracious permission of Her Majesty The Queen.

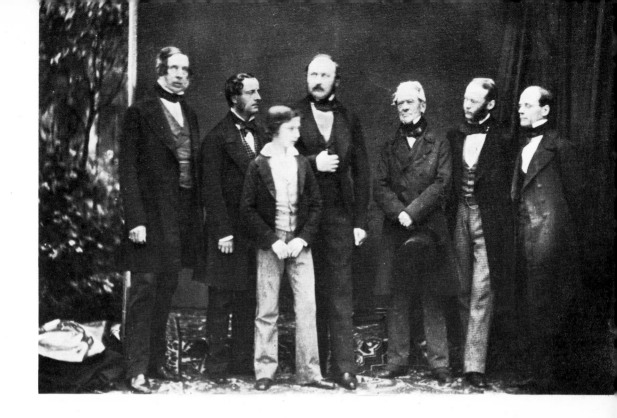

. . . a young, good-looking, amiable man [wrote the Prince], who
was a tutor at Eton. . . .

It is an important step, and God's blessing be upon it, for upon the
good education of princes, and especially of those who are destined to
govern, the welfare of the world in these days very greatly depends.

Even before Mr Birch took up his duties, the Prince of Wales –
then seven and a half – drew up a time-table for his work. He was
to spend six hours a day on religion and English, writing, French
and music, calculating, German, drawing and geography. To
this his father added: 'The Prince will not go to Church till he has
passed his eighth birthday, but the Tutor might on Sunday have
a short doctrinal exercise with him. . . . The Prince ought to say
his prayers morning and evening before the Tutor.'

In 1852, Mr Birch was followed by Frederick Waymouth
Gibbs, a Fellow of Trinity College, Cambridge. Gibbs was a
stern intellectual, and his pupil hated him. When the Prince of
Wales was seventeen, he was given a certain independence. He
passed from the hands of tutors to the care of a governor,
Colonel Robert Bruce (the brother of Lady Augusta). He was
also handed a memorandum which reminded him that life was
composed of duties, and that in their discharge 'the true Christian, true soldier and true gentleman' could be recognized. The
memorandum was signed 'V.R. and A.', but there was little
doubt who had drafted it. The Prince of Wales showed it to the
Dean of Windsor, and burst into tears.

The photographs show a sensitive boy, unhappy and withdrawn. However well his parents understood their other children, they consistently refused to understand him. 'Be not over
solicitous about education', Lord Melbourne had said.
' . . . It may mould and direct character, but it rarely alters it.'
The Prince of Wales, like his mother, was not an intellectual – but
he was sent to three universities. He spent a few terms at
Edinburgh, Oxford and Cambridge. However, he was not
allowed to lead the normal life of an undergraduate. His companions were a handful of selected dons and clergymen. When
Commemoration approached at Oxford, his father reminded
him: 'I trust you understand that the Balls etc., etc. which you
visit are not visited by you for your amusement but to give
pleasure to others by your presence.' Work, he reminded his son,
'is the only road to happiness, and I want to see you happy.'

In a private conversation with Lord Clarendon, which Lord Clarendon luckily recorded, Prince Albert confessed that he and the Queen might have been mistaken in their aggressive treatment of the Prince of Wales. He said that the task of punishment had always fallen on him, and that he did not resist the Queen's harshness towards her children because he was afraid of exciting her if she were thwarted. Greville had some justification for saying that the Queen 'does not much like' the Prince of Wales; after her husband died, she felt what Lord Palmerston called 'unconquerable aversion'.

Strangely enough, the relations between Prince Albert and his son seem to have been deeply affectionate. Some years after his father's death, at a Royal Academy dinner, the Prince of Wales tried to speak of him, and wept. In his first speech as Edward VII he referred to 'my father – ever to be lamented, good and wise'.

When the Queen and her husband returned from Scotland to Windsor, in the autumn of 1842, one figure from the past had disappeared. Lehzen's moon had long been on the wane. On 5 October Greville recorded that she had left the Castle.

> She is gone abroad for her health (as she says), to stay five or six months, but it is supposed never to return. This lady, who is much beloved by the women and much esteemed and liked by all who frequent the Court, who is very intelligent, and has been a faithful and devoted servant to the Queen from her birth, has for some time been supposed to be obnoxious to the Prince, and as he is now all-powerful her retirement was not unexpected.

Lehzen had gone for ever. She retired to Bückeburg, near Hanover, and there she died in 1870, surrounded by pictures of the Queen.

With the departure of Melbourne and Lehzen the Prince became virtually the Queen's private secretary. He prepared the papers which she was to see, made comments on them, and kept a record of everything that passed through his hands. He drafted almost all the Queen's important letters to Ministers, and recorded every conversation which he or she had had with members of the Cabinet. He compiled memoranda, filed and marked newspaper cuttings. As Mr Roger Fulford observed, in his life of

Prince Albert, he raised the business side of the monarchy to the dignity of a Government department.

Never was German industry so evident. In his diligence, as in his tastes, Prince Albert remained a Coburger all his life. Nothing about him was English, except the uniforms and orders which he wore, and his papers of naturalization. He looked German, and he spoke German to the Queen – a habit which did not endear him to the Court. Anson boldly reproved him for always speaking German, on the ground that his English did not improve. ('Nothing pleases here', noted the Queen, years later, '– more than speaking English with people – be it ever so little.')

And yet, in 1842, Prince Albert felt convinced that he was accepted in England. On 25 November he talked to Anson about the English dislike of foreigners. It was a curious conversation. The Prince was deluded, and his secretary was clearly diplomatic.

Queen Victoria's Christmas tree and presents, Windsor Castle, 1850. Watercolour, by J. Roberts. Reproduced by gracious permission of Her Majesty The Queen.

> I admitted [wrote Anson] it was quite true that a very laudable and natural jealousy and dislike prevailed in the minds of Englishmen against foreigners,. . . but with regard to *him* personally I did not think this spirit was at all prevalent. The Prince replied that he did not think Englishmen in general would pretend to any concealment of this national prejudice; but he must say with regard to himself, that he did not feel he was regarded in this spirit. On the contrary, every effort had been used to show him the kindest feelings, and to prove to him that, as the Queen's husband, he was looked upon as a thoroughbred Englishman.

He and his wife spent Christmas at Windsor. A big Chrismas tree – 'the German Christmas-tree and its radiant candles' – was set up in her private sitting-room, and a second tree was set up in the Oak Room for the Household. Charlotte Canning, a lady-in-waiting, reported: 'We had a great deal of feasting at Christmas in the way of very enormous meats & pies & German trees with sugar plums & presents given to every body. I have had my bracelet with the Queen's picture, really a nice thing to have.'

On 27 December, in the midst of the feasting and Christmas trees, Prince Albert retired to his study, and surveyed the scene with German earnestness:

My dear Stockmar,

... I cannot let the old year close without praising the foresight which during its course has arranged so much for my advantage, and without again seeing in the results a sacred duty, zealously to use the position I have been placed in for the good of all around me. ...

We have reached a critical transition period, in which seeds with a noble purpose may daily be sown. Still I feel the necessity for the wise counsel and support of a man of experience. When you left us, you said to me, 'When you really want me, write, and I will come'. I am well aware of what you are to your family, and your own concerns, and I have therefore been unwilling till now to importune you to return so soon. But the moment is come, when I think I may venture to remind you of your promise.

Prince Albert's mind (his biographer would write) 'has been by some called un-English. It had at least the peculiarly English quality of being practical.' He wanted Stockmar to help him to reorganize the Royal Household.

When Stockmar began his investigations, he found unbelievable muddle. Four Officers of State, the Lord Steward, the Lord Chamberlain, the Chief Commissioner of Woods and Forests and the Master of the Horse, were responsible between them for the fabric, service, catering, staff and heating of the palaces. Housemaids were under the control of the Lord Chamberlain, footmen were directed by the Master of the Horse, and the cooks took orders from the Lord Steward. If the Queen wanted a fire to be lit, two departments were involved. Certain traditions had become long-standing abuses. Every day fresh candles were placed in all the living-rooms, and, whether or not they were used, they were removed next day and became the perquisites of the footmen. Then there were forty housemaids at Windsor, and another forty at Buckingham Palace; they all received board and lodging and £45 a year for six months' work. Footmen were employed in relays: one-third were on duty, one-third on half duty, and the remainder were resting.

The Prince studied Stockmar's memorandum and carried out reforms. The Master of the Household was put in charge of all departments, and the Household was put on a budget. The Prince reduced the staff, he reduced their wages, he put an end to absurd perquisites and payments for long obsolete services. He was criticized for his economies, which sometimes verged on meanness. But waste, he decided, 'the canker of all, but especially of all great, establishments, should be made as difficult as possible, at the same time that nothing was spared which was essential for the befitting splendour of a great Monarchy.'

The New Year, 1843, opened gaily with two dances, and Lord Melbourne stayed again at Windsor. But the glamour had faded, and the Queen knew it. She *'almost* fancied happy old times were returned; but alas! the dream is past.' She still wrote to Melbourne frequently, she consulted him about the children's education, about Bertie's position as Prince of Wales, about political matters, even about the Speech from the Throne at the opening of Parliament. But Melbourne was fading from her mind, and she saw him less and less. 'Talked afterwards over former days', she wrote in her journal. 'My unbounded affection and admiration for Lord Melbourne, which I said to Albert I hardly knew from what it arose, excepting the fact that I clung to someone and having very warm feelings. Albert thinks I worked myself up to what really became quite foolish.' Albert was intent on breaking her links with the past.

The Queen's third child, Princess Alice, was born on 25 April 1843, and the Queen thought it would be friendly to ask her Uncle Ernest, the King of Hanover, to be a godfather. There were risks, for no one knew how he would behave. In fact the King behaved badly. He arrived for the christening in a four-wheeler, after both the christening and the luncheon were over, and he was annoyed that they had not waited for him. 'But', the Queen wrote, 'he was very gracious for *him*'. The graciousness did not extend to Albert. The King invited him to come for a walk in the London streets. Albert suggested that the crowds would be embarrassing. 'I used to be much more unpopular than you,' replied the King, 'but I used to walk about with perfect impunity'. Soon afterwards King Whiskerandos left English shores for ever.

Victoria and Albert returned to untroubled domesticity and art. This summer, in view of the decoration of the new Houses of Parliament, there was an exhibition of prize cartoons in Westminster Hall. There had been much investigation into the process of fresco painting – a genre which the Prince much admired. In order to encourage it, he commissioned a series of frescoes, based on Milton's 'Comus', to decorate a pavilion in the grounds of Buckingham Palace. Among the artists employed were Landseer, Maclise and Leslie, Uwins, Dyce and Stanfield. Uwins recorded how the Queen and Prince would come unannounced, unattended, twice a day, and watch the artists at work. In many things, he wrote, they were an example to the age. 'They have breakfasted, heard morning prayers with the household in the private chapel, and are out some distance from the Palace, talking to us in the summer-house, before half-past nine o'clock – sometimes earlier. After the public duties of the day, and before the dinner, they come out again, evidently delighted to get away from the bustle of the world to enjoy each other's society in the solitude of the garden. . . . Here, too, the royal children are brought out by the nurses, and the whole arrangement seems like real domestic pleasure.'

It was this summer that the Queen went abroad for the first time; and, on the new yacht, called – inevitably – the *Victoria and Albert*, she and her husband paid a visit to Louis-Philippe, King of the French and father-in-law of King Leopold. Since the accession of George III no English Sovereign had set foot on foreign soil, except when George IV had gone to his second Coronation at Hanover.

On 28 August the royal party drove from Windsor to Farnborough, where they got into 'the railroad carriage, which was fitted up for the occasion, & had a great crown at the top.

Crowds lined the road at every station,' Lady Canning wrote, 'and we caught a glimpse as we passed at full speed of rows of faces not so easily distinguished as the roadside poppies, & heard cheers drowned by the railroad noises. The Queen & Prince set to work to read the contents of 3 red boxes.' From Southampton they sailed to the Isle of Wight. They landed at East Cowes, and went to Norris Castle (where the Queen had stayed more than once as a child). 'Everything about it the Queen remembered, & kept constantly comparing it with the Pavilion, to the disadvantage of the last, & regretting she had not bought it when it was to be sold.' They sailed on to Plymouth. Lady Canning's ears were ringing with the thunder of royal salutes, 'which we had undergone about 15 times during the day. The Queen', she recorded, 'minds saluting when she is very near & gives orders that no firing shall ever take place when she is on board. This had happened to her once long ago & she said "we had to submit to it then, for we were not the greatest people." '

She was among the greatest, now.

At eight o'clock on the morning of 3 September [wrote an English biographer of Louis-Philippe], the royal squadron came in sight of the battery at [Tréport]. Repeated discharges of ordnance during the day, announced the still nearer approach of the august visitor, until five o'clock in the afternoon, when the deafening roar of hundreds of guns proclaimed the news that the squadron was at anchor off the port. Summoned by this tremendous voice of salutation, Louis-Philippe and his family left the Château [d'Eu, nearby], in carriages and on horseback, for Tréport, to receive their royal guest. . . .

Queen Amelia, Madame Adelaide, and the princesses, took their station on the pier-head, while Louis-Philippe, inspired by both personal and patriot gallantry, entered the royal barge, and directed his crew to pull for the bark that bore the Queen of the Ocean. In twenty minutes His Majesty was standing on the deck of the royal yacht of England – an event that was celebrated by a discharge of artillery, which enveloped the whole fleet, and harbour, and shore in one dense cloud of smoke for several minutes. . . .

The moment on which the two sovereigns stepped together on the soil of France, was hailed by loud shouts of *Vive la Reine, vive Louis-Philippe*, followed by renewed discharges of heavy ordnance, the deafening tones of which subsiding, were succeeded by the English anthem of *God Save the Queen* played by the band of the Carabiniers.

As the Queen reached the Château d'Eu, the sound of the national anthem was drowned by the cheering of the soldiers. At the banquet that followed, the dinner-service, brought from the Tuileries, was mostly of gold; and 'along the centre of the table extended a plateau of that precious metal, supporting golden vases and urns filled with aromatic plants and richly coloured flowers. Forty persons sat down to table, which number included the suite of her Britannic Majesty.' Among them was Lady Canning, who noted: 'Our Queen did not know what to do with her great French loaf.' She knew, however, instinctively, how to endear herself. The Duchess of Orleans – the widow of the King's eldest son – had not appeared in public since her husband's tragic death in a carriage accident; and she was not present at the banquet. Queen Victoria understood 'the best approaches to her aching heart, and availed herself of that knowledge by visiting the young princes in their nursery'.

The Queen's domestic behaviour was exemplary; and an English clergyman observed with approval that Sunday was devoted 'to those duties from which not even the Lord's anointed are exempt'. On Monday morning, however, the Queen sent early for Lady Canning. 'A band of 50 men was playing under the Queen's window & almost deafened her.' There followed a *fête champêtre*, a banquet, and private theatricals, performed by actors from the Opéra-Comique, in Paris. 'Reviews, drives round the vicinity of the Château, and visits to the tombs of the Guises, filled up the hours of the few days that were passed at Eu by the royal visitors.' On Thursday morning, at nine o'clock, Queen Victoria entered the state char-à-banc. It was presumably the one which Lady Canning found 'a mixture between one of Louis XIV's time and a marketing cart from Hampton Court'. It was drawn 'by 8 Wouwerman-like fat jumping horses, very much caparisoned'. In this astounding vehicle, the Queen returned to Tréport; and there she embarked in the royal barge for the *Victoria and Albert*.

On 15 September Mr Greville reported that the Queen's visit had gone off 'with complete success, and she left a good impression. . . . Aberdeen had a great deal of conversation with Louis-Philippe and with Guizot, mostly on the affairs of Spain.'

Queen Isabella of Spain was now thirteen years old, and the question of her marriage would soon arise. As usual, the House of Saxe-Coburg had a prince to offer: Leopold, the younger brother of Ferdinand, Prince Consort of Portugal. The Queen and Albert supported him; but France did not want a Coburg marrying yet another Queen, and Louis-Philippe proposed a family alliance of his own. He suggested that his son, the Duc de Montpensier, should marry Isabella's sister, the Infanta Fernanda. That did not suit the English politicians, for should anything happen to Isabella, Fernanda with a French husband would succeed her as Queen. A compromise was reached. It was informally agreed that Prince Leopold should not be the English candidate, and that Montpensier should not marry Fernanda, until the Queen had married some other non-Coburg prince and had had children.

The *Victoria and Albert* crossed the Channel to Brighton, where (reported Lady Canning) 'the beach was thronged with people & even the shallow water was full of boys & bathing women wading about. . . . The Queen is quite unhappy to leave the yacht, & to have to live in a house again; she says it feels like a prison, & she longs to be at sea.' However, the royal children were staying at the Pavilion, and Pussy was 'amazingly advanced in intellect, but alas also in naughtiness', Bertie was much *embelli*, and Alice (who was called Fatima because of her plumpness) was flourishing. A few days later, the Queen and her husband set sail again, this time for Ostend, to stay with King Leopold. He was delighted with their visit to his father-in-law; personal contact, he was sure, would banish any idea that the King of the French was astute and scheming. Louis-Philippe's geniality had in fact produced precisely the effect that he had intended.

For the rest of the autumn of 1843, the Queen and her husband paid visits to great country houses in England. Their progress, the Prince reported, was 'one unbroken triumph'. They stayed with the Duke of Devonshire at Chatsworth, where they much admired the vast conservatory, built by the Duke's head gardener, Mr Joseph Paxton. They stayed with the Duke of Rutland at Belvoir. 'At Chatsworth', wrote the Prince to Stockmar, 'there was a large and brilliant assemblage of the leading Whigs, and at Belvoir of the fashionable hunting men of Melton and Leicester. Here I took part in a regular fox-hunt, had a capital run, and moreover distinguished myself by keeping well up with the hounds all through. . . .' 'How well Albert's hunting answered!' wrote the Queen to King Leopold. The Press thought more of his seat on a horse than of his splendid speech to the manufacturers at Birmingham.

The Prince, had they known it, was also a fine shot. He skated well, and when the frost held he organized ice-hockey matches with members of the Household. When there was snow, startled Londoners might see him driving the Queen, the Princess Royal and the Prince of Wales in an elegant sledge down the Fulham Road. When the weather was bad, the Prince took his exercise on a velocipede. In the summer he used to swim in the Thames at Windsor. He played indoor tennis at Hampton Court, and skittles in the gardens of Buckingham Palace. Critics who dismissed him as a pure intellectual could not have known his accomplishments as a sportsman.

He did not choose to publish them, or to take this way of making friends among the sporting set. He did not stay at country houses for week-end shooting parties, any more than he troubled to belong to a London club, or to give a dinner-party for his own sex. He did not linger over port. He did not smoke (and 'the use of tobacco for smoking purposes' was prohibited at Windsor by royal command). The Prince had no time for small talk, or for social compliments. He showed a heavy lack of interest in women. 'Albert', wrote the Queen, 'is seldom much pleased with ladies or princesses.' Albert was in fact horrified by the thought of flirtation, let alone by promiscuity. Perhaps the profligate conduct of his father and brother had made him almost inhumanly high-minded. But one sometimes feels that sexual relations meant nothing to him but the performance of marital duty.

If the Prince was friendless, he had indeed only himself to blame. In social life he was singularly ungracious. He shared the German prejudice against the English aristocracy. He openly criticized English ways. He had a certain arrogance which he did not control. As his brother explained: 'Of mankind in general he was contemptuous.' It was not the way to win affection.

At the same time, he was acutely concerned about his public image, and – even in those days – about the publicity which was given to the Royal Family. He complained to the Duke of Bedford that whatever they did at Court, 'or were about to do,

Queen Victoria and Prince Albert on the frozen pond at Frogmore. Coloured lithograph, c. 1840.

was known. The Duke told him . . . that the world was curious to know and hear about them, and therefore the Press would always procure and give the information.' The conversation, recorded by Mr Greville, has a curiously modern ring.

The Queen herself was unaware of any imperfections in her husband. She had been delighted when, in the autumn of 1843, he had received the degree of Litt. D. at Cambridge. She saw how warmly the rising generation received him. But that, of course, was only natural, for 'Albert always *fascinates* people wherever he goes by his very modest and unostentatious and dignified ways'.

One wonders if the Queen really believed that her husband exercised this universal fascination. Perhaps – as E. F. Benson wrote in his *Queen Victoria* – she was too emphatic in her declarations. Or perhaps she was so convinced of his perfection that she could not conceive that other people would not recognize it. Sometimes her domestic happiness so overwhelmed her that nothing else appeared of any consequence, and after a week's holiday at Claremont she wrote to King Leopold: 'God knows *how willingly* I would *always* live with my beloved Albert and his children in the quiet and retirement of private life.' She was honest and disarming. But there was something else. She was Queen of England as much as she was Albert's wife.

However, it was not surprising that she adored him. He was astoundingly handsome, and his character was noble and kind. He had a passion for knowledge, and an untiring industry in its pursuit. He had strong artistic tastes. He also had a sound financial sense. As father of the young Prince of Wales he administered the estates of the Duchy of Cornwall. They consisted not only of property there, largely tin-mines, but of land in Lambeth and Kennington, where the Duke of Cornwall was Lord of the Manor. Here the Prince showed both his business sense and his philanthropy. As Benson reminds us, he vastly improved conditions for the tenants, he built them flats with the unheard-of luxury of bathrooms. But whereas in 1841, on the Prince of Wales's birth, these estates were bringing in £16,000 a year, by the time he came of age in 1859, the annual income was £60,000 and £600,000 had been set aside. This sum paid for the purchase of the Sandringham estate. In 1846 the Prince appointed a council to administer the Duchy of Lancaster.

Prince Albert at the age of twenty-four, clad in medieval armour. This was the Queen's favourite portrait of her husband. Painting by Robert Thorburn, 1843-4. Copyright reserved.

The Prince had a flair for the handling of money and the management of property. In politics he was discreet and wise; and the Queen, so jealous of her sovereignty, was now dependent on him. He was sharing her very throne, because she now insisted on his sharing it. It was strange that such an intelligent man did not tire of her adulation. But Albert had certain feminine instincts; he enjoyed her unremitting worship. It did not make him vain. He simply worked harder to deserve it.

It was perhaps because he had such integrity and dedication that he had an iron streak in his nature. Posterity, wrote his brother Ernest, could never 'form an idea of the almost marvellous contrasts that slumbered in him. . . . His gentle amiability was really coupled with such a critical sternness as to be almost a psychological riddle. The great, self-sacrificing affection was sometimes changed into painful coldness. . . . It was his perpetual thought how to make men happy, and yet he could be very hard on an individual man.'

Ernest wrote from experience. Their father, the Duke of Saxe-Coburg and Gotha, had written to Ernest, suggesting that the Queen or Albert should give him an allowance. Ernest sent this letter to Albert. Albert was adamant. 'Always money and always money', he answered, when he returned it. 'The principles [Papa] reveals in it really sting one to the heart.' Then Ernest himself became involved in a love-affair, and his relationship threatened to ruin his health. Albert sent him an unbelievable letter. Although, he said, 'he would never curse him or take away the love he owed him as a brother', he proposed 'to leave him to perish in immorality.' He cancelled the invitation he had sent him to visit England. 'Nothing would be more disagreeable at present than your visit.' He advised him to marry a virtuous wife, and to purify himself in the eyes of the world. To Albert – who was 'seldom much pleased with ladies or princesses' – it did not matter that one of them should sacrifice herself to a childless marriage. Ernest would have a wife, and his disgrace would be forgotten. Ernest took his brother's advice, and married Alexandrina of Baden. 'Ernest's marriage', wrote the Queen, 'is a *great, great delight* to us; thank God! I say, as I so ardently wished it.' Ernest spent his honeymoon at Claremont.

'To my mind,' wrote Prince Albert, 'the exaltation of Royalty is possible only through the personal character of the Sovereign.' Even before his betrothal he had framed the principles that must govern his own behaviour. He must remain beyond reproach, beyond the very suspicion of scandal. One of his self-imposed rules was never to be seen alone. All his movements must have the sign of official sanction. And so, as Sir Charles Grey was to write in *The Early Years of the Prince Consort*, 'wherever he went, whether in a carriage or on horseback, he was accompanied by his equerry. He paid no visits in general society.'

With his equerry, however, he was widely seen.

> His visits were to the studio of the artist, to museums of art or science, to institutions for good and benevolent purposes. Wherever a visit from him, or his presence, could tend to advance the real good of the people, there his horses might be seen waiting; never at the door of mere fashion. . . . He loved to ride through all the districts of London where building and improvements were in progress, more especially when they were such as would conduce to the health or recreation of the working classes; and few, if any, knew so well, or took such interest as he did, in all that was being done. . . . .
>
> Nothing [repeated a biographer] gave him greater pleasure than to be called upon to lay the first stone, or to inaugurate the opening of such institutions as baths or wash-houses for the poor in crowded neighbourhoods, industrial and ragged schools, and those more ambitious schools of art and design for the middle classes which have sprung up into active existence during the last ten years with such marvellous rapidity, and have been crowned with so much success. . . . To the Prince's fostering care and energy, the nation at large owes not a little of the vast improvement which of late years has changed most objects of ordinary manufacture, in point both of shape and of form. . . .

Nor was this all. In this *Life of the Prince Consort*, the anonymous author assessed the marriage of Victoria and Albert:

> We have been accustomed to look upon them as realizing that ideal of earthly happiness which, it is said, seldom falls to the lot of Princes. . . . For years he hardly ever stirred from the side of the Queen; and knowing how much the direction of a large family, the management of a great court, and the administration of public affairs must tax her strength, he gave her his help with an energy, an acuteness, a tenderness, and a solicitude of which there are few examples.

In the first years of their marriage Victoria and Albert had secured the moral dignity of their Court. They themselves already set a domestic example to Europe.

Early in 1844, on her return to Windsor, Lady Canning reported:

'The 3 children are quite darlings so very full of fun with such pretty manners; the little one is like a fat cottage child and the Princess Royal is rather thick & stout but grown since I last saw her & much prettier than she was. She has quite a royal memory & knew me & my name after four months absence. . . . The Prince of Wales now wears a little dress which I believe is like the Russian moujiks. . . . He looks very pretty in it.' Since the Queen herself danced country dances with animation, Lady Canning assumed that the family was not yet to increase. Seven months later, however, Prince Alfred – 'a very good specimen' – was born.

The New Year had opened, as usual, with dancing at Windsor. It also brought family mourning. On 29 January the Prince's father suddenly died. The Queen had only known him for two short periods, once when he came to England with his sons in 1836, and once when he attended her wedding. All the same, she assured King Leopold that it was an overwhelming blow. Duke Ernest had been a father to her, 'and his like we shall *not see again*'. She added a strange reflection for a blissfully happy wife: 'Indeed one loves to *cling* to ones grief.' Alas, this was to prove quite true hereafter.

Victoria's violent grief at the death of Duke Ernest was quite sincere, because he was Albert's father. It was true that Albert had not seen him for four years, and that in that interval he had found him exceedingly trying; but filial piety demanded that one should be brokenhearted. 'Here we sit together,' Albert wrote, 'poor Mama [the Duchess of Kent], Victoria and myself, and weep, with a great cold public around us, insensible as stone.' Even in the Victorian Age such sentiment was remarkable. When Queen Adelaide died, a few years later, Victoria wrote: 'We dined alone and after dinner talked of the funeral and of building a mausoleum for ourselves.'

Now, in the early days of 1844, she had a further reason for anguish. Albert wanted to go to Coburg, to be with his brother.

Queen Victoria and the Princess Royal. This is the first photograph of the Queen. Calotype 1844-5. Reproduced by gracious permission of Her Majesty The Queen.

Duke Ernest of Saxe-Coburg and Gotha, father of Prince Albert. Painting by Lowes Dickinson after Ruprecht. Reproduced by gracious permission of Her Majesty The Queen.

She could not go with him, and impose a Sovereign's presence in the house of mourning. After her marriage she had said that a parting between her and Albert '*will* and shall *never happen*, for I would go with him even if he was to go to the *North Pole*'. He was not going to the North Pole, but he was going to Coburg, and she would be left, inescapably, alone. The word had lost its charm since the early days of her reign. She now found solitude (or should one say independence?) unbearable. 'I have never been separated from him, even for *one* night', she explained to King Leopold, 'and the thought *of such* a separation is quite dreadful. . . . Still, I feel I could bear it – I have made up my mind to it, as the very *thought* of going has been a comfort to my poor Angel and will be of such use at Coburg. Still, if I were to remain *quite* alone, I do not think I *could* bear it quietly. . . . I may be indiscreet, but you must think of *what* the separation from my *all and all*, even only for a fortnight will be to me!'

King Leopold abandoned affairs of state in Belgium. He did not go to Coburg to show respect for his late brother. Instead he came to England with his wife. Victoria was parted from Albert for the first time. 'Poor child', he commiserated, from Dover. 'You will while I write be getting ready for luncheon, and you will find a place vacant, where I sat yesterday. . . . You are even now half a day nearer to seeing me again; by the time you get this letter you will be a whole one – thirteen more, and I am again within your arms.'

'I am again within your arms.' After four years of marriage, Albert still showed his feminine instincts, his strangely passive acceptance of devotion. The Queen looked up to him, in a sense, as *il mio padre*. She had always needed a paternal figure in her life. But the niece of George IV was physically passionate. Albert received the embraces, and Victoria bestowed them. 'Fortify yourself with the thought of my speedy return.' So he wrote to her. He sent her pressed flowers, gathered at the Rosenau, where he had been born; he sent her an auricula and a pansy from Reinhardtsbrunn. He was very fond of her; he recognized that their union was 'of heart and soul, and was therefore noble', but he did not yearn for her company, and he did not long for her embrace. His 'little grass-widow' longed for him; and, when he returned to Windsor, there was, so he recorded, 'great Joy'.

He plunged again into politics. He was much concerned about Ireland. Indeed, he had talked to the Duke of Bedford (to whom, said Greville, 'he seems to talk very openly') about 'the long course of misgovernment, and the necessity of doing something'. He had talked 'in such a strain that the Duke was convinced Peel had some serious intentions, or the Prince would never have said what he did.'

Albert was concerned with domestic politics, and with foreign affairs. Nicholas I of Russia invited himself to England this summer. He had an uncivilized mind, thought the Queen, he was sadly lacking in education and he was quite insensible to the arts, but he was very sociable, and the children were not shy of him. He was polite, he said of Windsor: 'C'est digne de vous, Madame'; and, best of all, he was full of praise for Albert, who had 'l'air si noble et si bon'. The Queen hoped that he would repeat these gratifying remarks abroad. There were friendly political talks, he wanted to be on good terms with England, 'but *not* to the exclusion of *others*'. As Benson writes: 'The French were clearly indicated; and the Queen hoped that they would not take this visit amiss, and endanger those cordial conversations with Louis-Philippe at the Château d'Eu, which she still thought had prevented any trouble over the Spanish marriages.' When the King of the French came to England later in the year he would, she told her uncle, have a 'truly affectionate reception'.

The Queen set great store by these royal visits, and they multiplied. With the Tsar came the King of Saxony. He was no problem at all, for he was '*so* unassuming,' and he went out sightseeing all day. In August came Prince William of Prussia, brother of the reigning King and later Emperor William I of Germany. Early in September, in Lady Canning's phrase, 'everything Royal that can be collected' came for the christening of Prince Alfred.

The Royal Family was, after all, beginning to grow *nombreuse*. It was fairly certain now that Albert's brother, the new Duke of Saxe-Coburg, would have no children, and so, after Ernest's death, Albert's children would succeed to the Dukedom. Bertie, as heir to the English Crown, could not inherit, and the new baby was the immediate heir. Alfred was an English Prince; but his father had not changed his allegiance. 'The little one', he assured the Duke, 'shall from his youth be taught to love the small dear country to which he belongs *in every respect*, as does his Papa.'

On 9 September, the christening over, the Royal Family set off for Scotland. They stayed at Blair Castle, in Perthshire, the seat of Lord Glenlyon, later Duke of Atholl. An exhausted lady-in-waiting reported: 'There is piping at 6 to wake us; the Queen's piper plays at 2 & the Albert piper at 6, & at guard mounting 2 pipes walk up & down playing for an hour.' The Queen rode her pony in the hills. The Prince shot a stag from the dining-room window. 'We are all well', he assured his stepmother, 'and live a somewhat primitive, yet romantic, mountain life, that acts as a tonic to the nerves. . . . Pussy's cheeks are on the point of bursting, they have grown so red and plump; she is learning Gaelic, but makes wild work with the names of the mountains.' And so the holiday continued. The Prince shot grouse, and the Queen sketched and painted, and on the hills they found a good spot for luncheon near a spring, and spread plates on the heather. Their tastes were simple. Lady Canning once advised her mother: 'If you do give a luncheon [for them] remember *cold beef*, that is always in favour. *No mutton.* Chickens, prawns & sand eels. No *onions*. . . . Seltzer water is the great necessity.' Yet perhaps Lady Canning was mistaken. Mr Roger Fulford tells us that the Prince disliked cold food. He introduced the habit of hot luncheons, and he insisted on interrupting his shooting to eat them.

The Queen and her husband left Blair on the last day of the month. She gave Lady Glenlyon a blue enamel and diamond bracelet; '& Albert', reported Lady Canning, 'gave us a little souvenir of himself, the teeth of a stag set like acorns with green enamel leaves'.

Victoria and Albert returned south to welcome yet another royal visitor. No King of France had come to England since 1356, when, after the Battle of Poitiers, Jean II – known as Jean le Bon – had been brought to Windsor as a prisoner of war. Louis-Philippe was now to come in state. On 7 October he embarked at Tréport. A few hours later, the *Gomer* docked at Portsmouth; and 'scarcely had an hour elapsed', wrote the King's biographer, 'when the illustrious Consort of Queen Victoria arrived, accompanied by the Duke of Wellington. . . . The moment the Prince stepped on deck, the yardarms became suddenly manned, the masts decked out with the gayest flags, and the band struck up the English national anthem. The effect was as instantaneous as a flash of lightning, or an electric shock, and could only have resulted from a combination of perfect discipline with ardent enthusiasm.' The King and the Prince went by carriage to the station, by train to Farnborough, and, again by carriage, to Windsor. 'And now the state carriages swept into the courtyard, and the foremost reached the castle-door, and the King descended with the buoyancy of fewer years to the vestibule. There the puissante Queen of this vast empire, her heart overflowing with kindness, extended both hands in token of enthusiastic welcome.'

The apartments prepared for Louis-Philippe were hung with crimson silk and blue, and the principal drawing-room was 'hung with the *chefs-d'œuvre* of Rubens'. Yet in Windsor, we are told, there appeared an instinctive appreciation of the Queen's wish 'that she should be allowed to receive her august guest in that private manner, that would best accord with his feelings on visiting England'. On the day of his arrival, the King was entertained in the private dining-room (it is true that 'the costly gold service' was used for the occasion). The following day

> was passed in viewing, in the most unceremonious manner, the grounds, gardens, buildings, and other interesting objects in the immediate vicinity of the Castle. Accompanied by his royal hostess, he promenaded on the terraces, visited St George's and Wolsey's chapels, and walked thence through the Home Park to the dairy and aviary. The confectionery, kitchen and gilt-room were also honoured by his presence. . . .

Early next morning, the char-à-banc which he had presented to the Queen drove into the quadrangle at Windsor, 'and the royal party entering it repaired to Twickenham, where His Majesty revisited the home of his exiled days'. There followed a tour of Hampton Court, luncheon at Claremont, a banquet at Windsor, and the King's investiture as a Knight of the Garter. There was a visit from the Lord Mayor of London, and a visit to Eton. Finally, the King sailed from Dover. He remained on deck until, in mid-Channel, 'a tremendous gale from the south-west com-

Queen Victoria and King Louis-Philippe setting out from Windsor Castle in the char-à-banc which he gave her, 10 October 1844. Watercolour by Joseph Nash. Reproduced by gracious permission of Her Majesty The Queen.

pelled him to go below'. He had endeared himself to the Queen, for he had warmly praised the Prince. 'Wonderful. . . . So wise. . . . He will always give you sound advice. . . . He will be like his uncle [Leopold], just as wise and just as good.'

The Prince himself was no doubt more pleased when the Prime Minister announced in Parliament that the Queen had entertained the Tsar and the King of the French without any expense to the country. She had paid for both State visits out of her private purse. Prince Albert's household reforms had borne fruit.

The Osborne Years

When the Queen and her husband had taken leave of Louis-Philippe, they sailed for the Isle of Wight. Victoria longed for more privacy than Windsor and Buckingham Palace afforded, for a house that should be 'free from all Woods and Forests and other charming Departments who really are the plague of ones life'. She had become engaged at Windsor, and she had spent her honeymoon there, but she had 'no feeling for Windsor. I admire it,' she was to write, 'I think it a grand, splendid place – but without a particle of anything which causes me to love it – none'. To her it was dull and tiresome and gloomy. Perhaps her feelings owed something to the fact that Albert now found Windsor 'devoid of enjoyment'. She herself ascribed her dislike to her unhappy childhood, to the tension between Windsor and Kensington. She thought 'of what I was always used to as a child. Always on pins and needles, with the whole family hardly on speaking terms. I (a mere child) between two fires – trying to be civil and then scolded at home! Oh! it was dreadful, and that has given me such a horror of Windsor, which I can't get over.'

As a small girl she had twice stayed with her mother at Norris Castle in the Isle of Wight, near Osborne Cottage, where Sir John Conroy lived. She liked the place, and in 1843 Sir Robert Peel had begun to make confidential enquiries about buying the Osborne Estate. Early in 1845, after her personal visit, the Queen bought some eight hundred acres, including Osborne House.

The house was not nearly big enough for the parents, the growing family, and the visiting Ministers, and the new Osborne House was at once begun. It was to be Italian in style. Albert designed it, with the help of Thomas Cubitt – the

architect to whom London owes much of its residential West End. He visualized the Clock Tower and the Flag Tower and the open colonnade, he laid out the grounds with their terraces and their 'blicks' of the sea. On 23 June 1845, the Queen laid the first stone of the Pavilion Wing.

The Prince was concerned with the outward appearance of Osborne House, and with the interior decoration. English sculptors, Thorneycroft and Theed and Boehm, produced more and more of the Albert Marbles. There was a lifesize group of the royal pair as Edward III and Queen Philippa – a commemoration of the costume ball. There was a statue of the Prince, incongruous in Roman armour, brooding, in an alcove, above the stairs. There were marble models of the royal children's hands and feet. The Prince considered fresco the noblest form of painting, just as he considered the organ the noblest musical instrument. So Mr Dyce, who had worked on the pavilion at Buckingham Palace, embellished the walls of the staircase at Osborne with an allegory of Neptune giving the empire of the sea to Britannia. On the walls of the Prince's dressing-room and bathroom he painted the marriage of Hercules and Omphale. Pictures by Winterhalter abounded. Winterhalter, the Queen told Lady Canning, 'has been most successful in the *Family Picture*, wh[ich] is universally admitted by all those who have seen it, to be one of the finest modern pictures painted, both as to composition & colouring, & the likenesses are most striking. It is in the style of a Paul Veronese. . . . He has likewise painted a beautiful little Picture of our eldest Boy in his Sailor's dress.' He was to paint Princess Helena, the Queen's third daughter, as an Amazon.

There were not only pictures by Winterhalter. There were paintings of dogs and horses by Landseer, and there were also 'porcelain views'. Famous or familiar scenes were painted under glaze on plates and teapots. Albert introduced this form of art from Germany. He and the Queen continued their etching; and in 1846 the Queen summoned Edward Lear to Osborne, to give her a course of twelve drawing-lessons. She made a deep impression on him. Nearly forty years later, he wrote: 'To my mind, [she] is one of the most remarkable women of this century or perhaps any other. . . . She is a true and fine woman in every respect. . . . I don't know if it is proper to call a sovereign a duck, but I cannot help thinking H.M. a dear and absolute duck, and I hope she may live yet thirty or forty more years, for every year she lives will be a blessing to her country.' One wonders what the Queen and the Prince would have thought of Lear's Nonsense; but they clearly admired his *Illustrated Excursions in Italy*. Prince Albert showed him a model of Osborne House, '& particularly a Terrace, saying – "This is what I like to think of – because *when we are old*, we shall hope to walk up & down this Terrace with our children grown up into men & women."'

On 15 September 1846, the new part of Osborne House was occupied for the first time. 'After dinner', recalled Lady Lyttelton, 'we were to drink the Queen and Prince's health as a house warming. And after it the Prince said very naturally and simply, but seriously: "We have a hymn in Germany for such occasions, . . . a prayer to bless our going out and coming in." And, truly, entering a new house, a new palace, is a solemn thing to do.' The house-warming had its gayer aspects: 'I forgot', she added, 'much the best part of our breaking-in, which was that Lucy Kerr [who was one of the maids of honour] insisted on throwing an old shoe into the house after the Queen, as she entered for the first night, being a Scotch superstition'.

Fortified by these introductions, Victoria and Albert settled into their new seaside palace. Neighbouring estates were added until the grounds covered more than 2,000 acres. The Household Wing was built in 1847–9, the Main Wing in 1849–51, and in 1853–4 a Swiss Cottage was imported, piece by piece, from Switzerland, and erected at Osborne for the royal children. In this delightful setting, wrote one of the Queen's biographers, 'youthful princes and princesses played at being men and women, practised the humbler duties of life, and kept natural history collections and geographical specimens, as their father and uncle had kept theirs at Coburg.' There were plots of ground – eventually nine in number – where they studied gardening in a practical manner. A journalist recorded that there were also 'greenhouses, hothouses and forcing frames, tool-houses, and even a carpenter's shop. Here the royal children used to pass much of their time. Each was supplied with a set of tools, marked with the name of the owner; and here they worked with the enthusiasm of an amateur and the zeal of an Anglo-Saxon. . . . Moreover, on this juvenile property was a building, the ground-floor of which was fitted up as a kitchen, with pantries, closets,

dairy, larder, all complete in their arrangements; and here might have been seen the young Princesses, floured to the elbows, deep in the mysteries of pastry-making.' Another delight (also borrowed from Coburg) was the miniature fort. Every brick of it was made, and every cannon founded, by the Prince of Wales and Prince Arthur.

As the reign continued, Osborne House became the very symbol of Victorian domestic felicity. We catch a glimpse of the Queen and Prince Albert, returning home from a state visit to France to find 'the sailor Prince, whose fourteenth birthday it

was, awaiting them on the beach. All the children, including the baby, were at the door. The dogs added their welcome. The young Prince's birthday-table was inspected. There was still time to visit the Swiss Cottage. . . . The children's castle, where they had lunched in honour of the day, was gay with flags. Prince Alfred with Princess Alice was promoted to join the royal dinner party. The little princes, Arthur and Leopold, appeared at des-

The Royal Family on the terrace at Osborne House. L. to R.: Prince Alfred, Prince Albert, Princess Helena, Princess Alice. Middle row Prince Arthur, Queen Victoria holding Princess Beatrice, the Princess Royal, Princess Louise. In front Prince Leopold, the Prince of Wales. Photograph by Caldesi, 26 May 1857. Reproduced by gracious permission of Her Majesty The Queen.

sert. "A band played", wrote the Queen, "and after dinner we danced, with the three boys and the three girls and the company, a merry country-dance on the terrace."' In winter, adds a biographer, 'the great household, like one huge family, rejoiced in the seasonable snow, in a slide used by young and old, and in a splendid snow-man.' Every New Year the royal children assembled at the Queen's dressing-room door to call (for the German influence remained regrettably strong): 'Prosit Neu Jahr!' Every year seemed happy in what the Prince called 'our island home. We are', he once wrote to a relative, 'wholly given up to the enjoyment of the warm summer weather. The children catch butterflies, Victoria sits under the trees, I drink the Kissingen water.' The Queen described her husband strolling through the Osborne woods, whistling to the nightingales 'in their own long peculiar note', or standing on the balcony at night to hear their song. Her journal records a gentle, unexpected side of his nature. He plays hide-and-seek with Vicky and Bertie, and even turns somersaults on a haystack 'to show Bertie how to do it'. Watching him with the children, she reflects: 'He is so kind to them and romps with them so delightfully, and manages them so beautifully and firmly.' Lady Lyttelton, a more detached observer, recorded him at Osborne, 'noisily and eagerly managing a new kite with his two elder sons'. She watched him as he helped to dress one of the smaller children, and decided: 'It is not every papa who would have the patience and kindness.' The Queen herself had patience, and gave her children religious instruction. The Archdeacon of London once told the youngest Prince: 'Your governess deserves great credit for instructing you so thoroughly.' 'Oh,' said the child, 'it is mama who teaches us'.

Edward VII gave the Osborne Estate to the nation. The state apartments and the Swiss Cottage, the museum and the gardens have long been open to the public. Now we may also visit the private apartments. To do so is to lose oneself in the Victorian Age. We enter the Prince's bathroom, see his enamelled bath in the alcove, his shower-bath surmounted by a massive head of Jupiter. We go on, into his study: sit at his writing-table, where the black-bordered notepaper, with its vignette of Osborne, the long slim envelopes and blue telegraph-forms, are waiting. Here is *The English Gentleman* which he was reading: 'Punctually at 12 o'clock the royal yacht was moored opposite to Osborne-house. . . . Her Majesty and Prince Albert disembarked from the royal barge and proceeded to Osborne-house in pony carriages.' Did the Prince carry, one wonders, that voluminous black umbrella or the ivory-handled one in the corner, and did he return to play the organ? 'Last evening such a sunset!' wrote Lady Lyttelton. 'From an open window below this floor began suddenly to sound the Prince's organ, expressively played by his masterly hand. Such a modulation! Minor and solemn and ever changing and never ceasing. From a *piano* (like Jenny Lind's holding note) up to the fullest swell, and still the same fine vein of melancholy. And it came so exactly as an accompaniment to the

sunset! How strange he is! He must have been playing just as the Queen was finishing her toilette, and then he went to cut jokes and eat dinner, and nobody but the organ knows what is in him, except, indeed, by the look of his eyes sometimes.'

We follow the Prince's ghost into the Queen's sitting-room: to the tables, side by side, where husband and wife shaped European policy, where despatches were held down by a paperweight in the shape of Eos, the Prince's greyhound, and the Queen's pen was dipped in this inkwell, in the shape of a sandalled foot. In the bookcase are Dean Stanley's *Sermons*, 'humbly offered by Mr John Murray', and under the window are miniature chairs once used by the royal children, the spinning-wheel at which their mother worked; in the corner is a musical box which still, today, plays Wagner.

In the Queen's dressing-room we see her bath and shower, the Minton toilet service which her husband gave her one Christmas; and in her bedroom we may inspect the busts of great composers along the mantelpiece, and Thorburn's portrait of the Prince in armour. In this bed, with another likeness of the Prince, in Garter robes, above her pillow, Queen Victoria died; and overhead is the bronze plaque 'in loving memory from her sorrowing children'.

The domestic, personal touch remains to the end. Though the Durbar Room still astonishes with its Hollywood opulence, the state apartment ceilings are still bright with 22-carat gold, the visitor to Osborne will be more moved by the private apartments – or, as Queen Victoria called them, the 'cheerful and unpalace-like rooms'. For here, every moment, on 'a real, brilliant Osborne day', one expects to see not a Queen and her Consort, but a husband and wife preparing to visit their Home Farm: a farm where they were so familiar that 'the tame pigeons would settle on his hat and on her shoulders'. 'I am writing in the lower alcove – with the deep blue sea as a background and the pleasant sound of the fountains soothing ones ears.' So the Queen told her eldest daughter, one July. 'Osborne', she wrote again, 'is really too lovely. . . . The deep blue sea, myriads of brilliant flowers – the perfume of orange blossoms, magnolias, honeysuckles – roses, etc. of all descriptions on the terrace, the quiet and retirement all make it a perfect paradise – which I always deeply grieve to leave.'

Queen Victoria's sitting-room, Osborne. Reproduced by gracious permission of Her Majesty The Queen.

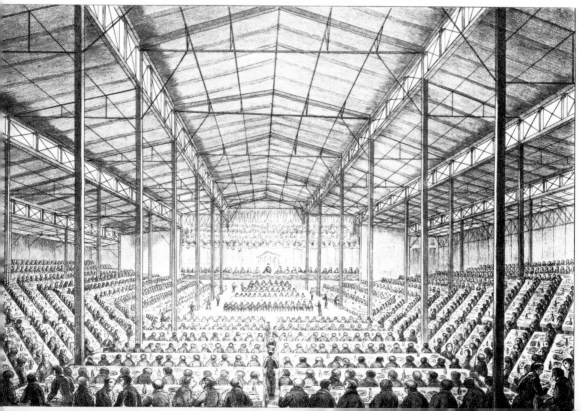

Osborne, added Lady Canning, 'perfectly enchants the Queen & Prince, & you never saw anything so happy as they are, planting their trees with the 5 babes playing around them.' Only one unfortunate incident marred the establishment of their new home. There was a herd of fallow deer on the estate, but it was thought that these would be destructive. The Prince arranged a *battue* in the worst German style, and they were all shot.

By the time the estate was bought, and the new house was furnished, the cost had been at least £200,000. The sale of the Brighton Pavilion in 1850 had furnished a fraction of the expense, but otherwise every penny was paid out of the Queen's private purse. So were the £70,000 which had been spent on the new stables at Buckingham Palace and Windsor. The Royal Family, it was observed, had 'set a unique example of cheerful and dignified economy'.

It has been said that, although he was not a conventional sportsman, Prince Albert had the country instincts of an English gentleman. He was certainly a countryman by nature. He warmly supported the Royal Agricultural Society; and at their annual meeting in 1848 he alluded to the company as 'we agriculturalists of England'. He could indeed claim to be one of them. At Osborne he described himself as 'partly forester, partly builder, partly farmer and partly gardener'. The Queen observed the pleasure he took in planting and transplanting trees (among them, alas, the hideous monkey-puzzle). He delighted in the creative aspect of gardening, 'seeing his work live and grow hour by hour'.

At Windsor – records Mr Fulford – he farmed some two thousand acres divided into three farms: Home, Norfolk and Flemish. He kept a herd of Herefords on the Flemish Farm and a herd of Devons on the Norfolk Farm. With unexpected humour, he named all the bulls after members of the Royal Family. One particularly fine animal was christened FitzClarence, after the illegitimate offspring of William IV. In 1844 the Prince won his first prize at Smithfield for pigs: the first of many. In 1850 he wrote: 'I am proud at having won a silver medal there for my fat pigs. For a cow I have only had honourable mention, and my sheep have received no notice at all.' In the late 1840s he began to bring the Windsor farms up to date. And, as a contemporary observed: 'That the Prince should have been one of the first persons in this country to appreciate the merits of Deep Drainage, to employ Steam Power in cultivation, . . . and to apply the resources of Chemistry to Practical Agriculture, ensured the welcome consequence that there would be many followers.' At Windsor he extended the Home Farm, rebuilt most of the buildings, and introduced modern agricultural machinery. He rebuilt the farmhouses and he put up a school in the Great Park. Agricultural labourers were to attend it in the evenings. He himself gave a Bible to each scholar.

On 13 December 1844, Lord Lansdowne and Lord John Russell went to Windsor. The first novelty that struck them, reported Mr Greville,

> was the manner of their reception. . . . Formerly the Queen received her Ministers alone; with her alone they communicated, though of course Prince Albert knew everything; but now the Queen and Prince were together, received Lord Lansdowne and John Russell together, and both of them always said *We* – 'We think, or wish, to do so and so; what had *we* better do, &c.' The Prince is become so identified with the Queen that they are one person, and as he likes business, it is obvious that while she has the title he is really discharging the functions of the Sovereign. He is King to all intents and purposes.

The Prince had succeeded in his aim. His domestic and political ascendency over his wife were now established, and both remained unchanged until his death.

The clearest idea of their relationship is found in a statement made by the Prince himself. It dates from the year 1850, but it was true five years before.

> While a female sovereign has a great many disadvantages in comparison with a King, yet, if she is married, and her husband understands and does his duty, her position, on the other hand, has many compensating advantages, and, in the long run will be found to be even stronger than that of a male sovereign.
>
> But this requires that the husband should entirely sink his *own individual* existence in that of his wife – that he should aim at no power by himself or for himself – should shun all ostentation – assume no separate responsibility before the public – but make his position entirely a part of hers, . . . continually and anxiously watch every part of the public business in order to be able to advise and assist her. . . . As the natural head of her family, superintendent of her household, manager of her private affairs, sole *confidential* adviser in politics, and only assistant in her communications with the Officers of the Government, he is besides the husband of the Queen, the tutor of the Royal children, the private secretary of the Sovereign and her permanent Minister.

This ponderous statement was made by Prince Albert, but the Queen approved it, and we may therefore take it as a joint summary of their relationship. If we accept that it was in fact a statement of their actual behaviour, then it is – at least in modern eyes – a total abdication. Never has any sovereign so renounced her rights as Queen or, indeed, as an individual. There was no area of her life, public or private, in which Queen Victoria did not act according to the will of her husband. The Prince implies that it was he who sunk his personality in hers. If we consider the Queen's recital of his perfections, we can estimate how formal was this sinking of himself in her, and how absolute was the sinking of herself in him. She records in her journal how she told him: 'It is you who have entirely formed me.' This was not true. She had been born with the instinct of sovereignty. She had been surpassingly royal, superbly independent. She had been educated as a future Queen, she had been schooled by Melbourne, and by her own experience. But, for Victoria, these years of married life were years of discipline. It is true that she learned from her husband how to curb her impatience and her impetuous judgment. It is true that he taught her a certain wisdom and that, during her marriage, her common sense was maturing, and her experience was widening. Happily her character still remained unchanged in these years of willing abdication.

Her recognition of her husband's rule was shown this year when she insisted to Sir Robert Peel that 'something must be done to place the Prince's position on a constitutionally recognised footing'. She would have liked him to be made King Consort – William III had, after all, reigned jointly with Mary II. But when Mr Borthwick asked in the House of Commons whether there was any intention of this, Peel denied it. 'Intention', he said, was too definite a word. The Queen was 'much hurt' at Mr Borthwick's impertinence, which was aggravated by the comments made in the Press, and by the suggestion that there was some idea of raising the Prince's income in proportion to his new dignity. 'Every imaginable calumny is heaped upon us, especially upon me', so the Prince had lamented to Stockmar. 'And although a pure nature, conscious of its own high purpose, is and ought to be lifted above attacks, still it is painful to be misrepresented.' Whatever the calumnies, and however the Prince was misrepresented, one fact remained inescapable: England did not want him as King Consort. Such was the hostility that the thought of a new title was, for the moment, abandoned.

Queen Victoria aged twenty-three. Painting by F. Winterhalter, 1842. Copyright reserved.

In mid-January 1845, the Queen and her husband stayed with the Duke of Buckingham at Stowe; and here – as at Osborne – the Prince indulged in an amusement which hardly won him English sympathies. The entertainments at Stowe began with *battues* in his honour.

> Fifty beaters [explained the Queen's biographer] . . . entered a thick cover and drove the game past the place where the sportsmen were stationed, into the open space of the park. Out the hares rushed from every quarter, so many of them that it was often impossible to stop more than one out of half-a-dozen. The ground immediately in front of the shooters became strewn with dead and dying. . . . The pheasants were averse to come and be killed, but at last quite a cloud ascended, and the slaughter was proportionately great.
>
> Slaughter, not sport, is the appropriate word.

On 18 January the Queen and the Prince returned from Stowe to Windsor. Two days later they set out again, this time to visit the Duke of Wellington at Stratfieldsaye. Prince Albert played indoor tennis with Lord Charles Wellesley, the Duke's younger son. But the bad weather, which kept him indoors, did not keep the public from trespassing, and the Duke was obliged to put up a notice in the grounds, 'desiring that people who wish to see the house may drive up to the hall door and ring the bell, but that they are to abstain from walking on the flagstones and looking in at the windows'.

The social round continued at Buckingham Palace, where, on 6 June, the Queen gave another fancy-dress ball. This one was known as the Powder Ball, 'because of the universally-worn powder on hair and periwigs.' Guests wore the costumes of 1740–50. The Queen herself was resplendent in 'a wonderful dress of cloth of gold and cloth of silver, with daisies and poppies worked in silks'. Her husband was superbly handsome in a crimson velvet coat edged with gold and lined with white satin, set off by the Order of the Garter. Miss Burdett-Coutts, the heiress, was also remarkable. Her diadem and necklace 'had once graced the brow and throat of poor Marie-Antoinette, and had found their way at last into jewel-cases no longer royal, owing their glittering contents to the wealth of a great city banker.'

In this summer of 1845, the Queen and her husband paid their first visit together to Germany; and here, once again, the Queen

Fancy-dress ball at Buckingham Palace, 6 June 1845. The guests wore dresses of George II's period. Watercolour by Louis Haghe. Reproduced by gracious permission of Her Majesty The Queen.

The Rosenau, where Prince Albert was born.

was reminded of the Prince's inadequate status. At Stolzenfels the King of Prussia gave precedence over him to the Emperor of Austria. But every slight was forgotten when she set eyes on Coburg, and on Albert's birthplace, the Rosenau. Albert had asked his brother not to spoil the visit by arranging too much ceremony; but on 21 August Lady Canning reported: 'We went into Coburg for the Queen to hold a sort of Drawing Room.' Next day, still at Coburg, there was a ball. 'I heard great approbation expressed at the Queen's hearty dancing, & I suppose she enjoyed it exceedingly as she allows herself to gallop, valse, & polk with her cousins, she went on incessantly till the ball ended.' The Duchess of Kent was in Coburg, and Baroness Lehzen came from Bückeburg to see her former charge. The Queen was delighted (and perhaps relieved) to find that Lehzen felt 'unchanged devotion'. But if Lehzen remained unchanged, the Queen, alas, did not. Or perhaps the Prince refused to let her show affection. On a later visit to Germany, their train passed through Bückeburg. Lehzen was waiting on the platform, waving her handkerchief. But the royal train did not stop.

Meanwhile, at Cologne, in the summer of 1845, there was a grand concert. It was conducted by Meyerbeer, who had composed a cantata in honour of the Queen. Jenny Lind sang, and for the first time the Queen heard 'the great singer, who, of all her sister singers, has most identified herself with England, and from her fine, womanly character and domestic virtues, endeared herself to English hearts.' The Swedish Nightingale endeared herself to Queen Victoria. Again and again, in London, the Queen attended her performances, and once, from the royal box, she cast her own bouquet at Jenny's feet. Jenny Lind was invited to Osborne, to sing duets with Lablache; and the Queen gave her a handsome bracelet, and said: 'I must again express, not only my admiration, but my respect for you.' The words were treasured still more than the gift.

Now, in 1845, on the way home from Germany, with Lord Aberdeen in attendance as Foreign Secretary, the Queen and the Prince spent a few hours with Louis-Philippe at the Château d'Eu, and they resumed their conversations about the Spanish marriages. Lord Aberdeen considered them satisfactory.

The winter of 1845–6 was darkened by the threat of political crisis. There had been a miserable harvest in England, and there was famine in Ireland, where the potato crop had failed. Peel believed that the only way to avert disaster was to repeal the Corn Laws; but his colleagues did not agree with him. In December he felt obliged to resign, and to recommend the Queen to send for Lord John Russell. As Benson observes, the prospect of losing her Tory Government now filled the Queen with as much despair as that with which she had once viewed their accession to power. And Melbourne could not help her now, for his health was broken. Worst of all was the prospect of having Lord Palmerston as Foreign Secretary: a post which he had held in two previous Governments. The Queen and her husband firmly believed that in foreign affairs the Crown had the predominant voice and indicated its wishes to the Foreign Secretary. Palmerston knew that as long as the Foreign Secretary was in office and his measures were endorsed by the Cabinet, the Crown was obliged to accept them. Palmerston at the Foreign Office was unthinkable, and the Queen tried to persuade Lord John to give him some less crucial post. However, any direct intervention of hers was averted, for Lord Grey refused to serve in the prospective Cabinet if Palmerston was given the Foreign Office; and, without Lord Grey's support, Lord John could not form a Government. So Peel withdrew his resignation, and the Queen turned to him to save her from the Whigs and Lord Palmerston. Peel now earned the superlatives which she had once showered on Lord Melbourne, and she assured King Leopold of 'my *extreme* admiration of our worthy Peel, who shows himself a man of unbounded *loyalty, courage*, patriotism and *high-mindedness*'.

One fact, at least, had triumphantly emerged from the crisis: the perfect conduct of the Queen herself. On 27 December 1845, *The Examiner* observed: 'In the pranks and bunglings of the last three weeks, there is one part which, according to all report, has been played most faultlessly – that of a Constitutional Sovereign. . . . Never, we believe, was the heart of a monarch so warmly devoted to the interests of a people, and with so enlightened a sense of their interests.' Prince Albert was delighted by such a tribute. On 6 January he wrote to Stockmar:

I believe that the crisis, now past, has been a source of real advantage to the Crown, by producing a widely spread feeling that amid all the general confusion and heat of party at least one person has remained calm and free from party spirit, this person being the Queen. The very Radical *Examiner* had a very remarkable article on the subject, in which it brought prominently forward the advantage for the country of a third power so free from partisanship. Our travels on the Continent, too, have made the impression general, that the *personal* appearance of the Sovereign in foreign countries assures the friendship of those countries for the English nation.

Alas, the rejoicing was premature. In June 1846 Peel was heavily defeated on the Coercion Bill for Ireland, and Lord John Russell became Prime Minister with Palmerston as his Foreign Secretary. The royal forebodings were confirmed. Before he had been in office a month, Palmerston sent an impatient despatch to the English representative at Madrid, without submitting it to the Queen. He complained of the delay in choosing a husband for Queen Isabella of Spain, and he mentioned three possible suitors. Among them was Prince Leopold of Coburg. The Queen and Lord Aberdeen had promised not to support Leopold, and the mention of his name gave the French the opportunity for the *coup* which Louis-Philippe had had in mind. The English had broken their engagement; his part of it was therefore no longer binding. It was instantly arranged that Isabella should marry her cousin Francesco, Duke of Cadiz, and that on the same day Montpensier should marry the Infanta Fernanda, now aged fourteen. The beauty of this arrangement was that Francesco was believed to be impotent. Montpensier would therefore probably become the father of the future sovereigns of Spain. Queen Isabella defeated this move by giving birth to five children. Possibly the Duke of Cadiz was more of a man than they had thought.

Queen Victoria was furious with Louis-Philippe, who had broken his word. Her temper was hardly improved by a letter from Queen Marie-Amélie, asking for her congratulations on the marriage of her son. 'You can', wrote Victoria, 'easily understand that the abrupt announcement of this *double marriage* could cause us nothing but surprise and very lively regret.'

Meanwhile, in the summer of 1846, Victoria continued to delight in her own domestic felicity. Before they moved into

Osborne House on 16 September, she and her husband made their last yachting excursion of the season. They sailed round the Cornish coast, and, from time to time, they landed to inspect the Duchy which was the apanage of their eldest son. Victoria set a bold example to contemporary women, and visited the Restormel iron mines. As her biographer noted:

> She was one of the comparatively few ladies who have ventured into the nether darkness of a pit. She saw her underground subjects as well as those above ground, and to the former no less than the latter she bore the kindly testimony that she found them 'intelligent good people'. . . . The Queen and the Prince got into a truck and were drawn by the miners into the narrow workings. . . . [The Queen] was not deterred from getting out of the truck with the Prince, and scrambling along to see the veins of ore, from which Prince Albert was able to knock off some specimens.

Prince Albert had now found yet further fields for his activities. None was too small to cultivate, and none was too large. He noticed, for example, that many posts in the Church of England – like cathedral canonries – were sinecures; he felt that they might be given to scholars who were engaged on research. The former student of Bonn University was now a Doctor at Oxford and at Cambridge. He was determined to promote education.

On his visit to Cambridge he had made such a favourable impression that, when the Chancellor of the University died, the Master of Trinity, and other Heads of Houses, asked him to stand for the Chancellorship. He agreed to do so, provided that there was no contest. As it happened, St John's – a powerful college – had already put forward a strong Tory and Church candidate, Earl Powys. Such was the feeling against the Prince in Tory Church circles that Earl Powys refused to withdraw.

The election aroused strong feeling. The London Press was solidly behind Earl Powys, and *Punch* ridiculed the sycophancy of the dons and their adulation of the young Prince of twenty-seven. The poll was held on 25, 26 and 27 February 1847. The Earl ran special trains from London for his supporters; but the Prince was elected by a majority of eighty, and on 27 February Mr Greville found the Court 'in high spirits'. The Prince was installed as Chancellor in July, and the installation went off, said Greville, 'with prodigious *éclat*, and the Queen was enchanted at the enthusiastic reception she met with'. Bishop Wilberforce agreed. 'There was such a burst of loyalty, and it told so on the Queen and Prince. . . . It was quite clear that they both felt it as something new that he had earned, and not she given, a true English honour; and so he looked so pleased and she so triumphant.' There was a great dinner in Trinity Hall, and, late that night, the Queen and her husband wandered on the banks of the Cam, 'Albert in his dress-coat with a mackintosh over it, I', wrote the Queen, 'in my evening dress and diadem. . . . All was so pretty and picturesque, in particular the one covered bridge of St John's College, which is like the Bridge of Sighs at Venice. We stopped to listen to the distant hum of the town; and nothing seemed wanting but some singing, which everywhere but here in this country we should have heard. A lattice opened, and we could fancy a lady appearing and listening to a serenade.'

Prince Albert was determined not to be a mere ceremonial figurehead. He invited the Master of St Catherine's to Windsor, and they discussed university reforms. The Prince deplored, in the strongest terms, that geography, modern languages, the history of art and aesthetics were not included in a Cambridge education. The Master agreed. Dr Philpott, the Vice-Chancellor, was also believed to be sympathetic to change.

> My dear Vice-Chancellor [wrote the Prince on 14 October],
> . . . I feel desirous of being furnished with a comprehensive table, showing the scheme of tuition in the Colleges separately and in the University for the ensuing year. I mean the subjects to be taught in the different Colleges, the authors to be read there, the subjects for examination, those selected for competition and prizes, and the lectures to be given by the different professors in their different branches. . . .

No doubt Dr Philpott was relieved when, soon afterwards, he retired from office. On 11 December the Prince assured his successor, Dr Phelps:

> I have received your communication about the Chancellor's medals for this year. I shall with pleasure continue these prizes, and even meditate adding a fourth for an *historical essay*. . . . In the absence of all historical lectures this stimulus to the study of history appears to me of some importance. . . . In the meantime the decision about the subject for the English poem presses. . . .

In the autumn of 1848 Prince Albert noted in his diary: 'My plan for a reform of the syllabus at Cambridge is carried by a large majority.'

In all Cambridge matters the new royal Chancellor took the most meticulous interest. As a foreigner, educated abroad, he could not understand the relative unimportance of professors and the extreme importance of college life. But his idea of a university was large and liberal. As he wrote to Lord John Russell: 'The Universities should not only be considered as schools and places for teaching and being taught, but also as seats of learning where the *savants* of this country may find a home which at present is absolutely denied to them, and they themselves being driven to join the money making pursuits or to starve.' The Chancellor of Cambridge might have written better English; but nowhere did he show to greater advantage than he did in his guidance of the University.

Education and enlightenment were, to him, the panacea for all the troubles of the world. 'I think further', he wrote to Lord John Russell, in the autumn of 1847,

> that *this* is the right moment and opportunity for correcting a great many misapprehensions existing about the object of English policy in general, and of setting this in its true light before the world. . . .
> My notion is this: –
> England has, by her own energies and the fortunate circumstances in which she has been placed, acquired a start in civilization, liberty, and prosperity over all other countries. Her popular institutions are most developed and perfected, and she has run through a development which the other countries will yet in succession have to pass through. England's mission, duty, and interest, is to put herself at the head of the diffusion of civilization, and the attainment of liberty. . . .
> Let her declare herself the protector and friend of all States engaged in progress, and let them acquire that confidence in England, that she will, if necessary, defend them at her own risk and expense. This will give her the most powerful moral position that any country ever maintained.

Prince Albert considered England's rôle in the world. He also understood the relationship between politics and social questions. He wanted to show that the Crown was aware of the problems created by the new industrial society. On 18 May 1848 he spoke to the Society for Improving the Condition of the Working Classes. His presidential address was wise and compassionate; and, despite its turgid style, it has its message for the twentieth century.

> The interests of classes too often contrasted are [said the Prince] identical, and it is only ignorance which prevents their uniting for each other's advantage. To dispel that ignorance, to show how man can help man, notwithstanding the complicated state of civilized society, ought to be the aim of every philanthropic person; but it is more peculiarly the duty of those who, under the blessing of Divine Providence, enjoy station, wealth and education.
>
> Let them be careful, however, to avoid any dictatorial interference with labour and employment, which frightens away capital, destroys that freedom of thought and independence of action which must remain to every one if he is to work out his own happiness, and impairs that confidence under which alone engagements for mutual benefit are possible.

The Prince showed his practical concern about the working classes when he helped to design Prince Albert's Model Houses for Families. These were built in pairs with a communal staircase. On the ground floor there were a living-room, scullery and lavatory; on the first floor were a parents' bedroom and two bedrooms for children. 'The *sleeping apartments*,' it was explained, 'being three in number, provide for that separation which, with a family, is so essential to morality and decency.' The model houses were first put up opposite the Crystal Palace, in connection with the Great Exhibition of 1851. 'His Royal Highness', went the report, 'has had this building raised on his own account, . . . to promote the much needed improvement of the dwellings of the Working Classes, and also to stimulate Visitors to the Exhibition, whose position and circumstances may enable them to carry out similar undertakings.' The detailed estimated cost of the model block of four houses was £458.5s.6d.

In this praiseworthy venture Prince Albert had employed the architect Henry Roberts; and Roberts recalled his 'remarkable appreciation of minute details. . . . This little structure [in Hyde Park] gave to the movement [for working-class housing] an impulse such as it has not received from any other single effort, the results of which have spread far and wide.' Sir Theodore Martin, the Prince's biographer, wrote later: 'The Prince believed that a mighty change would be initiated, if men of kind hearts and sound business heads could be persuaded to invest their capital in providing on reasonable terms homes for the sons of labour. . . . His views on the subject, regarded at first as somewhat Utopian, have since become accepted truisms.'

In the year 1848 it was clear that the working class must be contented if political stability was to last. There was revolution on the Continent. In February there was insurrection in Paris, and Louis-Philippe was obliged to abdicate, and to escape to England. He was much to be pitied, thought the Queen, especially as his misfortunes were largely of his own creation. He and his wife lived at Claremont, their son-in-law's house, for the rest of their lives.

The news of the February Revolution gave an impetus to the Chartists in England. Chartism was a militant movement among the working classes. The Reform Bill of 1832 had not given them the vote; they were still not enfranchised, and they felt increasing discontent at their living and working conditions. There had already been riots; now the news of the revolution in Paris led to a parade of Chartists in the streets of London. All the Chartist leaders had been released from jail, and a plan of action was drawn up. There was to be no violence, but a mass meeting was to be held on Kennington Common, and a procession of demonstrators was to take a petition for reform to the House of Commons. The date of the demonstration was to be 10 April 1848.

Queen Victoria – like the great majority of her contemporaries – did not understand democracy. As Mrs Woodham-Smith has said, in her life of the Queen, one of the very few criticisms that can be made of her is that she was not deeply concerned with improving the conditions in which most of her subjects passed their lives. As a young girl she had not been lacking in humane and generous impulses; but such impulses are apt to pass away with adolescence, and she had a tendency towards absolutism. Besides, at an impressionable period in her life, she had come under the influence of Melbourne: a man in whom a touching capacity for tenderness was allied to a dislike of reform and an almost entire want of sympathy for the masses. Queen Victoria lived through an era of profound social change, but neither public health, nor housing, nor the education of her people, nor their representation, engaged much of her attention.

Now, in the spring of 1848, she and her husband were alarmed by the thought of the Chartist gathering. So indeed was the Government. Martial Law was proclaimed, and two days before the great demonstration was due to be held, the Royal Family, with the lately born Princess Louise, removed themselves to Osborne.

The demonstration passed without violence. The National Petition was taken to the House of Commons, and the vast crowd quietly dispersed. Chartism was dead. 'Thank God!' wrote the Queen, 'the Chartist meeting & procession has turned out a complete failure; the loyalty of the people at large has been very striking & their indignation at their peace being interfered with by such wanton & worthless men – immense.' 'All is well with us,' wrote the Prince to Stockmar, 'and the Throne has never stood higher in England than at this moment.'

Europe, however, remained in ferment. There was insurrection in Austria and Italy, and the Prince recognized that the general peace might at any time be endangered. The surest way to avert disaster seemed to him to prove to the troubled nations that the prosperity of each depended on the prosperity of all. The world's progress was indivisible, and England must demonstrate the fact. There must be a vast International Exhibition in London. The Exhibition, so the Prince declared, must give the world 'a true test and a living picture of the point of development at which the whole of mankind has arrived, . . . and a new starting-point from which all nations will be able to direct their further exertions.' Academic and detached, the Prince ignored the factor of human passion; but he initiated the great international exhibitions which have, ever since, encouraged industrial progress and the expansion of trade.

He began by presenting his scheme to the Society of Arts, over which he presided. When they approved, he brought all his powers of organization to bear on it. The first step was to recruit English manufacturers and captains of industries. A dinner was held at the Mansion House, at which he addressed the mayors of eighty-two industrial towns in the provinces; he secured the municipal support of local centres. But England was only the foundation of the structure which he meant to raise. He wanted all foreign nations to join this progressive industrial fellowship.

Then opposition sprang up in England. It was largely directed against the Prince himself, and an organized attack was launched in the Press and in Parliament. Mistrust, resentment and dislike: Prince Albert was to inspire them all his life. But he worked on, the Queen supported him, and so did the industrial centres. He won financial support, and Parliament sanctioned the site which had been chosen in Hyde Park. Albert turned back to the designs which had been submitted for the building. One of them especially took his fancy. He remembered Mr Paxton's conservatory at Chatsworth. It was three hundred feet long and sixty-four feet high, so that the tropical trees inside did not even reach the roof. Both the Queen and the Prince had thought it 'out and out the finest thing imaginable of its kind'. Mr Paxton had now submitted a similar design on a far vaster scale. He suggested a glass conservatory a thousand feet long: a conservatory so high that the site would not need to be cleared of trees. Ruskin dismissed the building as 'the cucumber frame between two chimneys'; but Paxton's design was accepted.

The future looked bright; the past was slowly fading. On 24 November 1848 the Queen heard of the death of Lord Melbourne. 'Truly and sincerely', she wrote, 'do I deplore the loss of one who was a most disinterested friend of mine, and most sincerely attached to me. He was, indeed, for the first two years and a half of my reign, almost the only friend I had, except Stockmar and Lehzen, and I used to see him constantly, daily. I thought much and talked much of him all day.'

Melbourne had schooled her in politics. He had recognized her as a natural Sovereign. He had also recognized her husband's distinction. 'Lord Melbourne', noted Lord Clarendon, after the Prince's death, 'once told me that Prince Albert was the most remarkable young man he had ever met with in any rank of life. He was constantly adding to his knowledge, and never tired in pursuit of truth. . . . I [myself] never withdrew from his presence without feeling that I had acquired some knowledge, and brought away matter for reflection. . . . Such a conjunction of the choicest gifts of nature with acquirements so extensive, and a nature so kind and gentle, have rarely been found in any man.'

Kind and gentle indeed. On 6 May he addressed a meeting of the Servants' Provident and Benevolent Society. 'Who would not feel the deepest interest in the welfare of their Domestic Servants?' So he asked with paternal solicitude. 'Whose heart would fail to sympathize with those who minister to us in all the wants of daily life, . . . who live under our roof, form our household, and are a part of our family?'

On 11 July 1849 this paragon of virtues found himself at Osborne, looking through his diary. 'Tomorrow to Winchester, to be present at the dinner of the College, and to give the Welsh Fusiliers new colours – a ceremony which demands a military speech; and on the 25th to Weymouth-on-the-Sea, to lay the foundation stone of the breakwater at Portland. . . .' Nor did he forget his Cambridge duties. The Chair of History had recently become vacant, and he had offered it, in person, to Mr Macaulay. Unfortunately Macaulay had refused it, on the grounds that the duties would interfere with the completion of his history. 'Sir James Stephen, by the request of the Prince, embodied in writing his views of the duties of the office. . . . These were found so satisfactory, that, after a personal interview with the Prince, he received the appointment.'

On 2 August the royal yacht, with Victoria and Albert on board, steamed into Cove Harbour, Cork, on the first royal journey to Ireland since the days of George IV. Queen Victoria's simplicity won all hearts. 'I would never', she wrote, 'have consented to say anything which breathed a spirit of intolerance. Sincerely Protestant as I have always been and always shall be, . . . I cannot bear to hear the violent abuse of the Catholic religion.' As she entered her Irish capital, a dove, 'alive and very tame, with an olive branch round its neck', was let down into her carriage. The Queen had brought four of her children to Ireland; she created her eldest son Earl of Dublin. 'Och, Queen dear,' cried an old Irishwoman, 'make one of them Prince Patrick, and all Ireland will die for you!'

On May Day, 1850, the Queen gave birth to her third son and seventh child. The fact that the day was also the Duke of Wellington's eighty-first birthday determined Prince Arthur's first name and, perhaps, his future profession. Wellington and Prince William of Prussia were his godfathers. But 'the child's full names', wrote Albert to Prince William, 'will be Arthur

Queen Victoria and Prince Albert arriving at Belfast during their visit to Ireland, August 1849. Watercolour by P. Philips. Reproduced by gracious permission of Her Majesty The Queen.

Queen Victoria and Prince Arthur. Engraving by G. Zobel after a painting by F. Winterhalter. Courtesy of the Trustees of the British Museum.

William Patrick Albert – Patrick for the Irish to show our gratitude for their friendly reception of us last year. Victoria's love', he added, 'has always insisted on my name to finish up with'. She later ordained that all male descendants of her House should be given Albert as their last name, and that all female descendants should be given the name Victoria.

5

'My Dearest Albert's Own Creation'

The Great Exhibition was to be opened on Prince Arthur's first birthday: 1 May 1851. As the date approached, preparations became intense. Industrial products arrived from every quarter of the globe, and, as soon as the Crystal Palace was ready, they poured into it. The peaceful influence of the arts was represented, too. There was a vast organ in the concert hall, there was a picture gallery, there were stained glass windows, casts of Greek statues and of Egyptian bas-reliefs. Alfred Tennyson – the Prince's favourite English poet – politely assigned the glory of the scheme to the Queen:

> She brought a vast design to pass
> When Europe and the scattered ends
> Of our fierce world did meet as friends
> And brethren in her halls of glass. . . .

Such compliments were pure formality. No one doubted that, in his address to her, the Poet Laureate praised the fulfilment of her husband's dream.

Even now, at the last moment, there were predictions of disaster. On 14 April, a fortnight before the official opening, Prince Albert felt obliged to assure the King of Prussia:

Mathematicians have calculated that the Crystal Palace will blow down in the first strong gale; engineers – that the galleries would crash in and destroy the visitors; political economists have prophesied a scarcity of food in London owing to the vast concourse of people; doctors – that owing to so many races coming in contact with each other, the Black Death of the Middle Ages would make its appearance, as it did after the Crusades; moralists – that England would be infected by all the scourges of the civilized and uncivilized world; theologians – that this second Tower of Babel would draw upon it the vengeance of an offended God.

I can give no guarantee against all these perils, nor am I in a position to assume responsibility for the possibly menaced lives of your Royal relatives. But I can promise that the protection from which Victoria and I benefit will be extended to their persons – for I presume we also are on the list of victims.

On 1 May 1851, Queen Victoria duly opened the first International Exhibition.

> The Park presented a wonderful spectacle [so she dashed off in her journal], crowds streaming through it, carriages and troops passing by quite like the Coronation day, and for me the same anxïety: no, much greater anxiety, on account of my beloved Albert. The day was bright, and all bustle and excitement.... A little rain fell just s we started, but before we came near the Crystal Palace the sun shone and gleamed upon the gigantic edifice, upon which the flags of all the nations were floating....
>
> The glimpse of the transept through the iron gates – the waving palms, flowers, statues, myriads of people filling the galleries and seats around, with the flourish of trumpets as we entered, gave us a sensation which I can never forget, and I felt much moved.... One felt, as so many did whom I have since spoken to, filled with devotion, more so than by any service I have ever heard.... God bless my dearest Albert, God bless my dearest country, which has shown itself so great today! One felt so grateful to the great God who seemed to pervade all and to bless all.

The return to Buckingham Palace was, thought the Queen, 'equally satisfactory, the crowd most enthusiastic, the order perfect. We reached the palace at twenty minutes past one, and went out on the balcony and were loudly cheered.' Buckingham Palace did not, of course, have the now familiar façade, which was designed by Sir Aston Webb as a memorial to Edward VII. The balcony was not the one which we know today. But it was, apparently, on the day of the opening of the Great Exhibition, that the Royal Family appeared on the palace balcony for the first time. 'That *we* felt happy, thankful,' continued the Queen, 'I need not say; [I was] proud of all that had passed, proud of my darling husband's success, and of the behaviour of my good people.... Albert's name is immortalized.'

Queen Victoria opening the Great Exhibition at the Crystal Palace in Hyde Park, 1 May 1851. Crown Copyright. Victoria & Albert Museum.

'The First of May 1851.' The 82nd birthday of the Duke of Wellington and the first birthday of his godson Prince Arthur. Prince Albert holds the plans of the Crystal Palace, which is seen in the background. Painting by F. Winterhalter. Copyright reserved.

Prince and Princess William of Prussia had brought their son Frederick William, aged twenty, to the opening of the Exhibition, and for the first time he set eyes on his future wife, the Princess Royal. On the evening of 1 May, there was another family occasion. The Duke of Wellington came to see Prince Arthur, his godson, 'our dear little boy. He came to us both at five', wrote the Queen, 'and gave him a golden cup and some toys, which he had himself chosen, and Arthur gave him a nosegay.' Winterhalter recorded the occasion. His picture has been called 'an *Adoration of the Magi* with only one Magus'. There was to be an engaging, if brief, relationship between Prince Arthur and 'the Duke of Wellikon', and the following year, on Waterloo Day, the Prince was sent to pay the Duke a visit. The Prince was two years old, and he was 'so happy and so good, . . . the pair walking all about Apsley House together'.

As for the Great Exhibition, from the day it opened until the day it closed, it was seething with delighted visitors. The Duke of Saxe-Coburg felt a brother's pride.

> None of the innumerable similar undertakings which were carried out could [he wrote] in any way venture on a comparison with that first London Exhibition. . . . The high nobility undertook the representation of England in a manner such as there has since been no occasion for. All their splendour and pomp was displayed as if it had been part of the Exhibition. Later Expositions have had a more *bourgeois*, more industrial character – this first in London was preponderantly aristocratic. At the opening, four thousand gala carriages appeared, and almost daily the nobility was to be met in all the departments. The Queen and her husband were at the zenith of their fame. . . .
>
> Prince Albert was not satisfied to guide the whole affair only from above; he was, in the fullest sense of the word, the soul of everything.

The Queen herself was 'quite beaten' with the beauty and vastness of the Exhibition. 'A fairy scene: the *greatest* day in our history. Many cried and all felt touched and impressed with devotional feelings. It was the *happiest, proudest* day in my life.' The Exhibition was Albert's own conception, and after two years of incessant work, two years of bitter problems, he had been triumphant. On 10 May Mr Greville noted: 'The Queen wrote a touching letter to Lord John Russell, full of delight at her husband's undertaking, and at the warm reception which her subjects gave her. Since that day all the world has been flocking to the Crystal Palace, and we hear nothing but expressions of wonder and admiration. The *frondeurs* are all come round, and those who abused it most vehemently now praise it as much.'

The season of the first Exhibition was full of gaiety, in which the Queen and her husband joined. The Prince was now ubiquitous. He attended the Royal Academy dinner, he presided at a meeting of the Society for the Preservation of the Gospel, laid the foundation stone of the Hospital for Consumption and attended the meeting of the British Association. On 4 May the Queen and the Prince went to a reception at Stafford House. On 16 May they went to Devonshire House, and saw Lord Lytton's comedy *Not so bad as we seem.* It was performed by Charles Dickens and other amateur actors in aid of the new Guild of Literature and Art: a society founded to help poor authors.

On 2 June, Rachel gave her first performance of the new season to a cosmopolitan London thronged for the Great Exhibition. On 7 June, *Adrienne Lecouvreur* produced its usual sensation: the dying Adrienne, shown 'with surpassing minuteness', was a portrait well suited to the morbid sentimentality of the mid-Victorians. Queen Victoria attended the second performance, and sent the manager to Rachel 'to express the gratification she had received' from 'one of the finest pieces of acting imaginable – such a refinement of feeling,' she thought, 'and expression of passion, love, and sorrow, and such a fearful way of depicting death – of the delirium produced by poison. I frequently felt tears in my eyes. *All* acted extremely well.' The Duchess of Gloucester engaged Rachel to perform at Gloucester House, and the Queen and Prince Albert arrived to join the 'small party of 100' and applaud the scenes (which Rachel 'did quite beautifully') from *Athalie* and *Andromaque.* And when, between the representations, Levassor sang *Le Palais de Cristal*, imitating an Englishman speaking bad French, even the originator of the Crystal Palace was 'kept in fits of laughter'.

On 13 June the Queen gave her third costume ball. On this occasion the guests had to wear Restoration dress. The Queen herself wore a dress of grey watered silk. It was trimmed with gold and silver lace, and ornamented with bows of rose-coloured ribbon, fastened by bouquets of diamonds. She also wore a small

diamond crown. Prince Albert sported a coat of orange satin, brocaded with gold, the sleeves turned up with crimson velvet, and a pink silk epaulette on one shoulder. The Duke of Wellington, now eighty-two, came in scarlet and gold Restoration uniform. Even the young Mr Gladstone was present, masquerading as a judge of the High Court of Admiralty in the reign of Charles II. 'His dress was copied from an engraving in the British Museum. . . . It is difficult', confessed Sarah Tytler at the end of the century, 'to realize the "grand old man" of today in a velvet coat turned up with blue satin'.

On 18 June Prince Albert wrote triumphantly to Prince William of Prussia:

> The crowds at the Exhibition are bigger each day. . . . On the financial side we naturally stand very well. Russia has sent her treasures, and is now very well represented. India also has sent a fresh consignment of treasures. The judges will have finished their labours in a few days, and everyone is agog to hear their awards. There are crowds of Germans in London; French also and other foreigners. We expect our Uncle Leopold here today. Ernest, Alexandrine and Ernest Wurtemburg left on the 12th. The day following we had our *bal costumé* of the Charles II period, which went off really very brilliantly and transported us quite into his times. Yesterday I presided at the Jubilee Meeting of the Society for the Propagation of the Gospel . . . Tonight I dine with the old Duke of Wellington for the Waterloo Dinner. . . .

In July he became the President of the Zoological Society (six years later he was also to become the President of the Horticultural Society).

Day after day, in the intervals of such festivities, the Queen herself returned to the Crystal Palace, and every visit confirmed her enthusiasm. The Court was in London in October for the closing of the Exhibition. There had been 6,200,000 visitors. Lord John Russell declared that the enterprise would give the Prince imperishable fame. The Queen replied that the year 1851 would remain the proudest of her life.

On the day after the Exhibition closed, a London preacher delivered his Sunday sermon on the momentous undertaking. 'The pulpit', he said, 'is not the place for human panegyric; but it is only justice, to acknowledge the merits of a Prince, who has given the nation such solid ground of praise; naturalized among us less by the forms of law, than by the adoption of the national *mind*; and directing the advantages of his position, and the activity of his intelligence, to the true glory of England.'

The financial results exceeded all expectations. Two hundred thousand pounds had been guaranteed, but the guarantors did not need to pay a penny. Instead, there was a profit of £186,000 – or 93 per cent over and above the sum guaranteed. When all accounts were settled, the Prince advised the Commissioners to buy thirty acres of land round about the present Exhibition Road. They acquired them for £50,000. This site was also to serve the cause of education. On it today are a galaxy of museums and cultural institutions including the Royal Albert Hall.

The Queen's love and admiration for her husband could scarcely increase, but – as Benson said in his *Queen Victoria* – she now extolled his gifts so high that she depreciated her own. He showed 'such perspicacity, such *courage*'. 'We women', she told King Leopold, 'are not *made* for governing – and if we are good women we must *dislike* these masculine occupations.' And again: 'I am every day more convinced that *we women* if we are to be *good* women, *feminine* and *amiable* and *domestic* are *not fitted to reign*.' It was a strange *volte face*. As a young girl, with Melbourne by her side, she had assumed her sovereignty with utter confidence and undisguised delight. She had been superbly independent. Now, with Albert by her side, and fourteen years of experience behind her, she reaffirmed her virtual abdication.

Two entrancing visits to Scotland had made the Queen determined to have a house of her own in the Highlands. Sir James Clark, the royal physician, had heard about the fine air of Deeside. He had urged her to acquire the lease of the Balmoral estate from the Earl of Aberdeen. On 8 September 1848, Victoria and Albert had stayed at the old Balmoral Castle for the first time. 'It is', wrote the Queen, 'a pretty little castle in the old Scottish style. There is a picturesque tower and garden in front, with a high wooded hill; at the back there is wood down to the Dee; and the hills rise all round. At half-past four we walked out, and went up to the top of the wooded hill opposite our windows. It was so calm, and so solitary, it did one good as one gazed around; and the pure mountain air was most refreshing. All

Interior, Crystal Palace. Reproduced by gracious permission of Her Majesty The Queen.

Gillies and foresters with stag shot by Prince Albert near Balmoral, 5 October 1854. Reproduced by gracious permission of Her Majesty The Queen.

seemed to breathe freedom and peace, and to make one forget the world and its turmoils.' A few days later, Prince Albert told the Dowager Duchess of Saxe-Coburg: 'We have withdrawn for a short time into a complete mountain solitude, where one rarely sees a human face. The snow already covers the mountain tops, and the wild deer come creeping round the house. . . . The air is glorious and clear, but icy cold.'

And so began a kind of life which demanded a Landseer to record it: indeed, to the Queen herself it seemed like an endless series of his paintings. 'A salmon', she wrote, 'was speared here by one of the men; after which we walked to the ford, or quarry, where we were very successful, seven salmon being caught, some in the net, and some speared. . . . The scene at this beautiful spot was exciting and picturesque in the extreme. I wished for Landseer's pencil.'

> Our people in the Highlands [wrote Albert] are altogether primitive, true-hearted, and without guile. . . . Yesterday the Forbeses of Strathdon passed through here. When they came to the Dee, our people offered to carry them across the river, and did so, whereupon they drank to the health of Victoria and the inmates of Balmoral in whisky, but as there was no cup to be had, their chief, Captain Forbes, pulled off his shoe, and he and his fifty men drank out of it.
>
> The deer are wild, and give me so wide a berth that I have only brought down four, and this after infinite trouble.

Victoria and Albert revelled in the remoteness and privacy of the place. They picnicked, they made incognito tours through wild parts of the Highlands, staying at remote inns and eating tough chickens without potatoes. They made friends with the gillies, and Lady Augusta Bruce, lady-in-waiting to the Duchess of Kent, remembered the Queen and her husband coming to visit the Duchess at Abergeldie, 'armed with an immense Gaelic dictionary as large as themselves, which they studied the whole time!' When the Queen was not out with the Prince, she took the crofters presents of flannel petticoats, and made small purchases in village shops. They lived like a conscientious homely couple on holiday, and Victoria delightedly exchanged the formal head-dress which she wore on London evenings for a simple wreath of Scottish heather. In 1849, Mr Greville was summoned to Balmoral for a Privy Council, and he was glad 'to have seen the

Queen and Prince in their Highland retreat, where they certainly appear to great advantage. The place', he recorded, 'is very pretty, the house very small. They live there without any state whatever. . . . There are no soldiers, and the whole guard of the Sovereign and the whole Royal Family is a single policeman, who walks about the grounds to keep off impertinent intruders.' After dinner, when the table had been cleared, the Queen and the Prince went back to the dining-room and learned how to dance Scotch reels. The Prime Minister and Mr Greville played billiards. Lord Aberdeen, noted Greville, 'said the Prince's views were generally sound and wise, with one exception, which was his violent and incorrigible German unionism'. When Albert was not discussing politics, he cast off his usual stiffness. He made puns. And, since his humour had not changed since his Coburg days, he roared with laughter if somebody tripped over a hearthrug. Lord Granville, who was known for his wit, used to say that he never told his best stories; it was much more effective to pretend that you had pinched your finger in the door.

The lease of the Balmoral estate ran for thirty-eight years from 1836, but the Queen and her husband could not bring themselves to give it up. Prince Albert bought the fee simple of it in 1852. The old Balmoral Castle was too small for them; and once again he himself turned architect. On 28 September 1853, the Queen laid the foundation stone of the new Balmoral Castle. On 7 September 1855, she and Albert stayed in the new castle for the first time. 'An old shoe was thrown after us into the house, for good luck, when we entered the hall. The house is charming: the rooms delightful, the furniture, papers, everything, perfection.'

The Balmoral estate remained romantic. At the end of the century Sarah Tytler, the Queen's biographer, recorded:

> Within the gate, the surroundings are still wild and rural, . . . and have a faint flavour of German parks where the mowing-machine is not always at work. . . .
> Great innocent moon-daisies, sprightly harebells, sturdy heather, bloom profusely and seem much at home within these royal precincts, under the brow of the hills and within sight and sound of the flashing Dee. . . .
> The house is built of reddish granite in what is called the baronial style, with a sprinkling of peaked gables and pepper-box turrets. . . .

Indeed, the Queen's Scottish castle somewhat resembled a German schloss.

Indoors, continued Miss Tytler, 'many a relic of the chase appears in antlered heads. . . . The engravings on the walls are mostly of mountain landscapes, and sporting scenes, in which Landseer's hand is prominent, and of family adventures in making this ascent or crossing that ford.' There was also an acknowledgment of the Queen's extremely distant Scottish ancestry.

> The furniture is as Scotch as may be – chairs and tables, with few exceptions, of polished birch, hangings and carpets with the tartan check on the velvet pile, the royal 'sets' in all their bewildering variety. . . .
>
> The corridors look brown and simple, like the rest of the house. . . .
>
> In the drawing-room is a set of chairs with covers in needlework sewed by a cluster of industrious ladies-in-waiting. In the library hangs a richly wrought wreath of flowers in porcelain, an offering from Messrs Minton to the Queen. . . .

Lady Augusta Bruce was a trifle more critical. 'There are', she reported,

> beautiful things – Chandeliers of Parian; Highlanders, beautifully designed figures, holding the light, and which are placed on appropriate trophies – table ornaments in the same style, and loads of curiously devised and tasteful, as well as elaborately executed articles; the only want is a certain absence of harmony of the whole. . . .
>
> The carpets are Royal Stuart Tartan and green Hunting Stuart, the curtains, the former lined with red, the same dress Stuart and a few chintz with a thistle pattern, the chairs and sofas in the drawing-room are 'dress Stuart' poplin. All highly characteristic and appropriate, but not all equally *flatteux* to the eye.

To the Queen herself it was all *flatteux,* and all to be admired. 'Every year', she wrote, 'my heart becomes more fixed in this dear Paradise, and so much more so now, that *all* has become my dearest Albert's *own* creation, own work, own building, own laying out, as at Osborne, and his great taste and the impress of his dear hand have been stamped everywhere.'

The Queen's admiration was loyally echoed, in years to come, by the Prince's official biographer.

To increase the comfort of his tenants, to elevate their moral and social condition, were objects steadily kept in view from the time the Prince became a proprietor of Highland property; and they were pursued with unabated zeal to the end of his life.

School-houses were erected and teachers appointed for the education of the young; and an excellent library, the joint gift of Her Majesty the Queen and the Prince, was established at Balmoral and thrown open to all in the neighbourhood. Houses and gardens, with a croft, where it could be more conveniently added, for the keep of a cow, were provided at a very moderate rent for the blacksmith, the carpenter, shoemaker, tailor, and general merchant. . . .

The Queen herself believed in good works, and visited the poor.

I walked out [she wrote] with the two girls and Lady Churchill, stopped at the shop and made some purchases for poor people and others, drove a little way, got out and walked up the hill to Balnacroft, Mrs P. Farquharson's, and she walked round with us to some of the cottages to show us where the poor people lived, and to tell them who I was. Before we went into any we met an old woman, who, Mrs Farquharson said, was very poor, eighty-eight years old, and mother to the former distiller. I gave her a warm petticoat, and the tears rolled down her old cheeks, and she shook my hands, and prayed God to bless me: it was very touching. . . .

If the Queen loved the Highlanders, it was soon clear that the Highlanders had come to love the Queen. And when she observed to a gillie that it must be very dull when the Family left, he answered: 'It's just like death come all at once.'

The Queen was happier at Balmoral and Osborne than anywhere else. Osborne had the Solent to cut it off from the outside world, but it was not so very far from London. Balmoral was delightfully inaccessible. Queen Victoria loved these weeks when she and her husband could at times forget their royal status. When, in 1868, she published *Leaves from the Journal of our Life in the Highlands*, a Victorian clergyman observed that, 'of all the days to which they refer, those were the most enjoyed, and the pleasure of them was most eagerly sought to be renewed, on which the Queen and her party could go forth in disguise, roaming among the hills and about the villages, unrecognized.'

We had decided [wrote the Queen] to call ourselves Lord and Lady Churchill and party, Lady Churchill passing as Miss Spencer, and General Grey as Dr Grey. Brown once forgot this, and called me

'Your Majesty' as I was getting into the carriage; and Grant on the box once called Albert 'Your Royal Highness'; which set us off laughing, but no one observed it. . . .

The mountains gradually disappeared, – the evening was calm, with a few drops of rain. On and on we went, till at length we saw lights, and drove through a long and straggling 'toun', and turned down a small court to the door of the inn. Here we got out quickly – Lady Churchill and General Grey not waiting for us. We went up a small staircase, and were shown to our bedroom at the top of it – very small, but clean – with a large four-post bed which nearly filled the whole room. Opposite was the drawing and dining-room in one – very tidy and well-sized. Then came the room where Albert dressed, which was very small. Made ourselves 'clean and tidy', and then sat down to our dinner. Grant and Brown were to have waited on us, but were 'bashful,' and did not. A ringletted woman did everything. . . . The dinner was very fair, and all very clean – soup, 'hodge-podge', mutton-broth with vegetables, which I did not much relish, fowl with white sauce, very good potatoes, besides one or two other dishes, which I did not taste, ending with a good tart of cranberries. . . .

[Next morning] evidently 'the murder was out', for all the people were in the street, and the landlady waved her pocket-handkerchief, and the ringletted maid (who had curl-papers in the morning) waved a flag from the window.

In 1884 the Queen published *More Leaves from the Journal of our Life in the Highlands.* She sent a copy to Tennyson, with touching diffidence. 'Its only merit', so she wrote, 'is its simplicity and truthfulness.'

Perhaps, as usual, she was right. But we should not underestimate the effect of these two books on her people. They showed her, the Queen of England, already a legendary figure, as an endearing human being. And they remind us, today, that if she had some of the sentimentality of her epoch, she also had its striking virtues. She believed unshakeably in a close domestic life. She was simple, religious, absolutely honest. She had great gusto and a sense of purpose. She had large reserves of physical and moral energy. And somehow, even as she rode her pony round the hills, and ate hotch-potch, incognito, at a little Highland inn, she was – as she alone could be – royalty in person.

Lord Palmerston's injudicious despatch on the Spanish marriages in 1846 had been the first of a series of frictional incidents.

Repeatedly – as Benson records – the Queen had reminded the Foreign Secretary that he had failed to show her the drafts of instructions to her Ministers before they were sent off. She asked that it should not occur again; and, alas, it did. Palmerston sometimes used language ill-befitting the 'calm dignity' which the Queen felt appropriate to the British Government. She was afraid that some day 'he might give her name to sanction proceedings which she may afterwards be compelled to disavow'. It was only right that the Queen should feel strongly about this. But Palmerston, on the other hand, considered that he was responsible for England's international relations. The Queen, however reluctantly, had entrusted him with that duty, and, provided that his views were approved by the Cabinet, he intended to behave as he chose. On this point, undoubtedly, Palmerston was right. He was just as clearly wrong in not getting the Queen's permission to act in her name, without ascertaining her views. He was also wrong if, having ascertained them, he modified them without consulting her. But Palmerston could countercharge the Queen with irregular practices. He ascertained that she had received a letter from the King of Prussia which the Ambassador had been told to deliver to her in person. It did not deal with private affairs, but with the English policy towards the unification of Germany under Prussia. This scheme was strongly favoured by the Queen herself and by her husband. Once she had read the letter, the Queen should of course have passed it on to her Foreign Secretary. Palmerston therefore insisted on reading it, and on dictating a non-committal answer. His action brought a personal element into the antagonism, and it embittered both parties. The Queen, the Prince and Lord John Russell discussed removing him from the Foreign Office. The Queen said that she distrusted him not only on matters of policy, but 'on personal grounds'. The Prince intervened; he suggested that she had not meant this. The Queen withdrew the word 'personal'. But she had meant exactly what she said. She had a violent personal objection to Palmerston; for, unlike Melbourne, Peel and Aberdeen, he had no respect for the Prince's opinions, and no patience with his endless memoranda. 'To me', the Prince once told the Queen, 'a long closely connected train of reasoning is like a beautiful strain of music.' To Palmerston, the Prince was a German pedant. To the Prince, Lord Palmerston was 'an able politician with large views and an energetic mind, an indefatigable man of business, a good speaker; but a man of expediency, of easy temper, no very high standard of honour and not a grain of moral feeling.' 'I cannot respect that man', he added, 'for he always prefers his own interests to those of the nation'.

To the Queen, any criticism of Albert was now virtual blasphemy. But Palmerston did worse than criticize him, he ignored him. He disagreed, understandably, with his views on international politics. Palmerston was a patriotic and determined Englishman. He refused, rightly, to encourage the unification of Germany under Prussia. He supported the Danish claim to the Duchies of Schleswig and Holstein.

The Prince's nerves had been strained by the preparation of his Exhibition, and, in the autumn of 1851, the Queen was not eager to leave the quiet of Balmoral for the turbulence of politics. Her apprehensions were justified. She and the Prince had hardly returned to Windsor when Palmerston devised a fresh embarrassment. Kossuth, the Hungarian revolutionist, had arrived in England, and Palmerston decided to receive him. There was a flurry of agitated letters between the Queen and the Prime Minister. The Queen took Lord John's advice; and, as Kossuth had made some violent speeches since his arrival, she forbade Palmerston to receive him. Lord John summoned the Cabinet to consider the situation. Palmerston bowed to their opinion, and promised that he would not receive Kossuth. But it is more than likely that he had already done so, for ultra-Radical meetings sent him notes of thanks for his 'courteous attentions' to the revolutionist, and the Queen told Lord John that she had '*every reason to believe* that he has seen him after all'.

The Prime Minister now found himself in a delicate position. The Queen still insisted that her husband was '*looked up to and beloved* as *I* could *wish* he should be'. Lord John was all too well aware that this was a pathetic fallacy. It was not the Prince who enjoyed enormous national popularity. It was Palmerston. And any Government which quarrelled with him risked its existence. Lord John was also aware, though he could never tell the Queen, that the Prince was more foreign than ever to the nation. Since he dominated the Queen, he was considered to be a far greater danger to the country than her headstrong Foreign Secretary.

There was now a brief respite from Palmerston. On 2

December 1851, Louis-Napoleon Bonaparte, the elected President of the French Republic, dissolved the National Assembly, gave himself full powers, and installed himself as Prince-President for ten years. It was only a matter of time till the Empire was restored. The Queen and the Government disapproved of the coup-d'état, and Palmerston was instructed to write to the British Ambassador in Paris that England was maintaining strict neutrality. Privately, however, he told Count Walewski, the French Ambassador in London, that he 'entirely' approved of the President's action. Count Walewski duly informed his Government that Palmerston approved, and England found herself in the awkward position of having declared both her approval and her neutrality. 'Lord John,' the Queen had written, once, 'has the power of exercising control over Lord Palmerston, the careful exercise of which he owes to the Queen, his colleagues and the country.' Lord John now asked Palmerston for an explanation, and, since it was unsatisfactory, he dismissed him from the Foreign Office. The Queen and the Prince were delightfully surprised. Needless to say, the Prime Minister was not rebuked for failing to ask Her Majesty's consent.

As Mr Roger Fulford writes in his life of Prince Albert, the significance of the long struggle between the Crown and Palmerston lies in the political power which the Prince secured for the Queen. In the first place, he established the right of the Crown to dismiss an individual Minister. It was the knowledge that the Queen and Prince intended to use this power which made Lord John himself dismiss Palmerston. Prince Albert was anxious to establish a further point. 'There was', he wrote, 'no interest of the House of Coburg involved in any of the questions upon which we quarrelled with Lord P. . . . Why are princes alone to be denied the credit of having political opinions based upon an anxiety for the national interests and honour of their country and the welfare of mankind?'

Two months after Palmerston's dismissal, the Government was defeated in the House of Commons. Lord John resigned, and the Queen called on Lord Derby to form a Ministry. The only interest about its transitory life was that Disraeli was Chancellor of the Exchequer. But in the winter the Derby Government was defeated over his budget. Lord Aberdeen then undertook to form a Coalition Government, but he could not do so without Palmerston. Within a year of his 'extinction,' the irrepressible politician re-entered the Cabinet as Home Secretary.

Meanwhile the indiscretion of approving the coup-d'état – for which Palmerston had been dismissed – was beginning to justify itself. Prince Albert sternly disapproved of Louis-Napoleon's morals, and the Queen had insisted on neutrality. But neutrality was likely to become more dangerous than indiscretion. There was to be a *Te Deum* in Paris to mark the beginning of the new régime. The Corps diplomatique was to be present. The Queen expressed her wish that Lord Normanby should not attend. She did so for the vindictive reason that, if he attended, Palmerston could say that, although his approval of the coup-d'état had caused him to lose his post at the Foreign Office, the Queen's Ambassador 'had been ordered publicly to thank God for its success'. But soon the Queen's sturdy common sense told her that England must establish good relations with France, and she explained to King Leopold that she intended to keep on cordial terms with the Prince-President. King Leopold approved, for Belgium was perilously placed. He felt like a traveller in the tropics who finds a snake in his bed, 'and must *not move, because that irritates the creature*'. Good relations with England would soothe the creature, and make it less inclined to bite Belgium. When the Prince-President duly assumed the title of Emperor, the Queen wrote to 'Sir, my Brother', and assured His Imperial Majesty of her invariable attachment and esteem.

Napoleon III was delighted by such acceptance. Indeed, he made a proposal of marriage to Princess Adelaide of Hohenlohe, who was the daughter of the Queen's half-sister, Feodora. He hoped to ally himself, albeit rather distantly, with the Royal House of England. The Queen did not like that, nor did Feodora, nor indeed did Adelaide. They were all relieved when the Emperor married Eugénie de Montijo.

The season of 1852 began, and it was particularly gay, a reflection of the general prosperity of the country. The King of the Belgians, interfering as ever, felt some apprehension that Victoria and Albert might even forget their duty in the pursuit of frivolity.

Allow me to say just one word about the London season [the Queen reassured him]. The London season for us consists of two State balls and two concerts. We are hardly ever later than twelve o'clock at night, and our only dissipation is going three or four times a week to the play or opera, which is a great amusement and relaxation to us both. As for going out as people do here every night, to balls and parties, and to breakfasts and teas all day long besides, I am sure no one would stand it worse than I should; so you see, dearest uncle, that in fact the London season is nothing to us.

The London Season ended, and the nation was bereaved. On 14 September 1852 the Duke of Wellington died. Invitations were countermanded, the Court went into mourning. Ships in the Thames and in all English ports flew their flags at half-mast, and garrison music was forbidden. 'One cannot', the Queen wrote, 'think of this country without "the Duke", our immortal hero.'

Baron Stockmar, whose faculties were clearly in decline, saw Prince Albert as the Duke's moral successor. 'Your appeal to me', wrote the Prince, 'to take the place of the Duke for the country and the world shall stimulate me to fresh zeal in the fulfilment of my duties. . . . I must content myself with the fact that constitutional monarchy marches unassailably on its beneficent course, and that the country prospers and makes progress.'

Not until Parliament reassembled could the Duke be granted the national funeral which he deserved. Two months elapsed between his death and his burial. In November the Queen, the Prince and their children saw his lying-in-state in the great hall of Chelsea Hospital. 'The Dear Queen', wrote Lady Augusta Bruce, 'felt much her last visit to Her faithful and best friend – Dear Princess Royal wept out loud, the darling, and everyone seemed overcome.' On 18 November the Duke was buried in St Paul's, by the side of Nelson. 'Our poor dear Prince' was present, and 'was perfectly overcome, . . . and the Dear Queen', continued Lady Augusta, 'could scarcely speak of it even as she heard it from him without tears. . . . [The Dear Queen] wears a bracelet with his hair.' The Queen and her children had watched the procession from the balcony of Buckingham Palace.

There was soon to be yet another child – the eighth – in the family. On 7 April 1853 the Queen gave birth to her fourth son. He was called Leopold (after the King of the Belgians), George

Baron Stockmar. Reproduced by gracious permission of Her Majest The Queen.

(after the King of Hanover), Duncan (as 'a compliment to dear Scotland'), and, of course, inevitably, Albert. He was baptized on 28 June.

A fortnight after Wellington's death, Prince Albert had assumed two of his appointments: Colonel-in-Chief of the Rifle Brigade, and Colonel of the Grenadier Guards. The post of Commander-in-Chief had also fallen vacant. The Duke himself had suggested that Prince Albert should succeed him; but he preferred not to do so, and Field-Marshal Viscount Hardinge was appointed. The Prime Minister must have been relieved at this decision. The Prince was not only foreign, he had had no military training. There would have been violent opposition to his appointment. Such opposition would have been all the more justified because war was imminent.

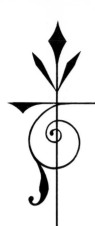

6

'He Governs Us in Everything'

On 22 June 1853 Russia invaded the Danubian principalities of Turkey. Ostensibly she meant to protect the religious rights of the twelve million Christians of the Orthodox Church; in fact she intended to establish her sovereignty. By the autumn this invasion produced the desired result. On 23 October Turkey – unequipped for war – declared war on Russia. England looked on the ocean as her private property, and she felt insulted when a Russian fleet destroyed a Turkish fleet at anchor in the harbour of Sinope. Napoleon III appealed to the Tsar for peace, and the Tsar replied by insulting him. The Powers moved ineluctibly towards conflict.

Lord Aberdeen explored every means of maintaining peace, but his Cabinet was divided. Palmerston (once again he was right) felt that England must go to war. As a protest against the dilatory behaviour of his colleagues, he resigned his seat in the Cabinet. No doubt he calculated that this would inflame the general belligerence. In fact it unleashed a storm of insults over the Queen and her husband. If Palmerston had resigned, Prince Albert must have been responsible; if the country remained neutral, that was because Prince Albert willed it so. Prince Albert was openly mentioned as the hostile influence behind the throne. He was charged with betraying English interests, and with working into the hands of foreign powers. He was attacked for his German birth, and for his connection with King Leopold. 'Above all,' said the *Daily News,* 'the nation distrusts the politics, however they may admire the taste, of a Prince who has breathed from childhood the air of courts tainted by the imaginative servility of Goethe.' It was said that the Home Secretary had

opened Prince Albert's letters and found him in correspondence with the Russians.

> You jolly Turks now go to work,
> And show the Bear your power
> It is rumoured over Britain's isle
> That AL is in the Tower;
> The postmen some suspicion had,
> And opened the two letters,
> 'Twas a pity sad the German lad
> Should not have known much better. . . .

So went a verse on a broadsheet: *Lovely Albert!* 'One word more', wrote the Prince himself to Stockmar, 'about the credulity of the public. You will scarcely credit, that my being committed to the Tower was believed all over the country – nay, even "that the Queen had been arrested!" People surrounded the Tower in thousands to see us brought to it!' 'You could not marry the Queen of England', Stockmar told his pupil, 'without meaning, and without being bound to become a political soldier. . . . It is only in war that a real soldier is formed.' Albert was indignant at the treatment he received, but the Queen was hurt. She wrote to Lord Aberdeen: 'In attacking the Prince, who is one and the same with the Queen herself, the throne is assailed.'

The Prince might write that Palmerston – or Pilgerstein, as he called him – was 'possessed by all his juvenile levity'. But before 1853 was over, the Cabinet had come round to Palmerston's view that war was inevitable. They much regretted his resignation, for Palmerston out of office was a political menace, and Palmerston in office was worth tens of thousands of votes. They opened communications with him. Before the end of the year, he withdrew his resignation. This helped to silence the allegations against Prince Albert. Although these allegations were ridiculous, the Prime Minister still felt obliged to deny them in public. They were condemned by the leaders of the Government and the Opposition in both Houses of Parliament. Before the end of February 1854, all negotiations with Russia broke down. England and France declared war on her.

During the Crimean War, it was clear that the Anglo-French alliance must be strengthened, and that the first step towards this was an understanding between the English Court and Napoleon III. In the summer of 1854 the Emperor was to camp with his

troops at St Omer. Prince Albert received 'a pressing invitation' to meet him there. Early in September, in the *Victoria and Albert*, the Prince sailed for Boulogne. On 4 September, as he approached the French coast, he snatched a moment to write to the Queen.

Dear little Wife,

    Whilst you sit at breakfast with the children, and are teased by the wasps, of which Arthur is horribly afraid, and makes grimaces at, I sit in the cabin at my table (yours is there empty), and wish you on paper a loving good-morning. The night was superb. After we had thrown you, by blue lights, a parting salutation, which you returned from the *Fairy*, following it by one last greeting under a flare of torches, which was left unanswered, we travellers sat upon deck till half-past eleven, in the glorious moonlight. It was close upon twelve when I got to bed in the cabin, which had a very blank and desolate look. . . .

    About ten we shall make the port, and I have to get myself into full uniform beforehand. Shortly afterwards some further news, my dear child! . . .

Prince Albert's visit to the Emperor
Napoleon III at St Omer,
5 September 1854. Watercolour by
George Thomas. Reproduced by
gracious permission of Her Majesty
The Queen.

Boulogne, half-past one o'clock.
. . . I have had two long talks with the Emperor. . . . People here are
far from sanguine about the results of the expedition to the
Crimea, . . . nevertheless, so far as the Emperor is concerned, determined to consider the war and our alliance as the one thing
paramount. . . .

Boulogne, 5th. Sept.: ten p.m.
. . . The Emperor thaws more and more. This evening after dinner I
withdrew with him to his sitting-room for half an hour before
rejoining his guests, in order that he might smoke his cigarette, in
which occupation, to his amazement, I could not keep him company.
He told me one of the deepest impressions ever made upon him was
when . . . he arrived in London shortly after King William's death,
and saw you at the age of eighteen going to open Parliament for the
first time.

The *entente cordiale* was established.

From the Crimean War we may date Prince Albert's attain-
ment of full political power. In the early years of his marriage he
had had to fight for the Queen to make him her partner in
politics. In the middle years of his life he had had to struggle with
the politicians. He had had to make them accord the Crown the
political position to which it was entitled by tradition and ability.
From 1855 onwards that position was recognized and enjoyed,
and an observer could write of the Prince: 'I take it that he
governs us really in everything.' The Queen herself admitted it.
A few years later, she observed to the Princess Royal: 'One great
advantage . . . you all have over me, and that is that you are not in
the anomalous position in which I am, – as Queen Regnant.
Though dear Papa, God knows, does everything – it is a reversal
of the right order of things which distresses me much and which
no one, but such a perfection, such an angel as he is – could bear
and carry through.' Once, when the Prince had been away, the
Queen told her daughter: 'I did my best during his absence – and
he was much pleased with my "stewardship".' It was a revealing
and, to some, regrettable comment.

With the wholehearted support of the Queen, the Prince was
now unofficial sovereign. Count Charles Frederick von Eckstädt
Vitzthum, the Saxon envoy, wrote that he was 'complete master
in his house, and the active centre of an empire whose power
extends to every quarter of the globe. It was a gigantic task for a

young German Prince to think and act for all these millions of British subjects. All the threads were gathered together in his hands'. With the support of the British Government, he had also begun to be a statesman: to become a European figure.

Throughout 1854 the war overshadowed all other interests. 'From the palace to the cottage, women's fingers worked eagerly and unweariedly knitting comforters and muffatees to protect the throats and wrists of the shivering men. We have heard', wrote Sarah Tytler, 'that the greatest lady in the land deigned thus to serve her soldiers. We have been told of a cravat worked in crochet by a queen's fingers which fell to the share of a gallant young officer in the trenches.' 'Her state about the Crimeans, and soldiers in general!' exclaimed Lady Augusta. 'She said the patient, grateful look of those in hospital went through her heart, and you can hear her enumerating the cases with the usual memory, and knowing the names and histories of each.'

The Prince had rightly not become Commander-in-Chief, but he still played a significant part in military affairs. He summoned a meeting at Windsor, and persuaded the Prime Minister, the Commander-in-Chief, and the Secretary of State for War to accept his plan for reorganizing the army in the Crimea. He complained that convalescent soldiers were being sent back to the Front before they had fully recovered. He urged that a convalescent camp should be established in Corfu. In the early months of the war he was much concerned with attempts to bring the army up to full fighting strength. In November 1854 he wrote to the Secretary at War, Mr Sidney Herbert, and urged that reserves for the Crimean army should be built up in Malta and Gibraltar. Broadly speaking, the Prince's suggestions were carried out, and there was a steady flow of troops for the fighting line. He was no less concerned about the conduct of military operations. The Government seems to have welcomed his suggestions, but they took care that the range of his activities should not be known.

Early in 1855, the outcry against the incompetence at Scutari led to Lord Aberdeen's resignation. An embarrassing fact had then to be faced. There was only one man in the country who could keep a Ministry together, and finally the Queen had to send for him. Palmerston accepted with alacrity.

He was as unpredictable, as disconcerting as ever. Within a week of taking office, he visited the Emperor in Paris, and blithely told the Queen that they intended to correspond. 'How,' enquired Prince Albert, 'how can the Foreign Secretary and Ambassador at Paris, the legitimate organ of communication, carry on their business if everything has been previously preconcerted between the Emperor and the English Prime Minister?' Palmerston shrugged his shoulders. He continued to dismiss such unnecessary strains of music.

In April 1855 the Emperor and Empress of the French were to pay a State visit to England. A splendid suite, including the Rubens, Zuccarelli and Vandyck rooms, was set aside for them at Windsor Castle. By an irony of fate, the Emperor's bedroom was the one that had been occupied by Louis-Philippe. The Queen herself was touched by a more pathetic reminder of events. Two or three days before the arrival of Napoleon III, old Queen Marie-Amélie had paid a visit to Windsor. 'It made us both sad', wrote Queen Victoria in her journal, 'to see her drive away in a plain coach with miserable posthorses, and to think that this was the Queen of the French, and that six years ago her husband was surrounded by the same pomp and grandeur which three days hence would surround her successor.'

On 16 April Prince Albert welcomed the Emperor and Empress at Dover. That evening, they arrived at Windsor.

> The band struck up 'Partant pour la Syrie', the trumpets sounded, and the open carriage, with the Emperor and Empress, Albert sitting opposite to them, drove up, and they got out.
>
> I cannot say [dashed off the Queen] what indescribable emotions filled me, how much all seemed like a wonderful dream. These great meetings of sovereigns, surrounded by very exciting accompaniments, are always very agitating. I advanced and embraced the Emperor, who received two salutes on either cheek from me, having just kissed my hand. I next embraced the very gentle, graceful and evidently very nervous Empress. . . .

The Queen was impressed by the Emperor's quiet manner. As for the Empress: 'She is full of courage and spirit, yet so gentle, with such innocence and *enjouement*, that the *ensemble* is most charming.' There were morning walks, and long conversations about the Crimea. There was a review of the Household Troops in the Great Park. There was also a ball in the Waterloo Room – French susceptibilities had, for once, been ignored. The Queen danced a quadrille with the Emperor, who 'danced with great dignity and spirit. How strange', she reflected, 'that I, the grand-daughter of George III, should dance with the Emperor Napoleon, nephew of England's great enemy, now my nearest and most intimate ally, in the Waterloo Room.'

It was strange indeed; and stranger, still, when she invested him with the Order of the Garter. Bishop Wilberforce, who was present, found him 'rather mean-looking, small, and [with] a tendency to *embonpoint*; a remarkable way, as it were, of swimming up a room, with an uncertain gait; a small grey eye, looking cunning, but with an aspect of softness about it, too. The Empress, a peculiar face from the arched eyebrows, blonde complexion; an air of sadness about her, but a person whose countenance at once interests you. The banquet was magnificent. At night', added the Bishop, 'the Queen spoke to me. "All went off very well, I think. . . . We put the riband on wrong, but I think it all went off well, on the whole." '

The visit could hardly have gone off better. The Emperor and Empress went to London, and attended a banquet at the Guildhall. They attended a gala performance of *Fidelio*. On 20 April, the Emperor's forty-seventh birthday, the Queen gave him a pencil-case, and Prince Arthur gave him two violets – the Bonapartes' flower. The Empress – 'your favourite Empress,' the Queen was to remind her – made the conquest of the Princess Royal. The royal and imperial party went to Sydenham, to see the reconstructed Crystal Palace. The Emperor and Prince Albert attended two war councils; the Queen herself attended the second, and found it 'one of the most interesting scenes I ever was present at. I would not', she wrote, 'have missed it for the world'.

The visitors finally left for France on 21 April.

Napoleon III was understandably eager to strengthen these cordial relations, and almost at once the visit was returned. He himself spent more than a fortnight supervising the preparations, and on 17 August he set out for Boulogne to greet Queen Victoria and her husband, the Princess Royal and the Prince of

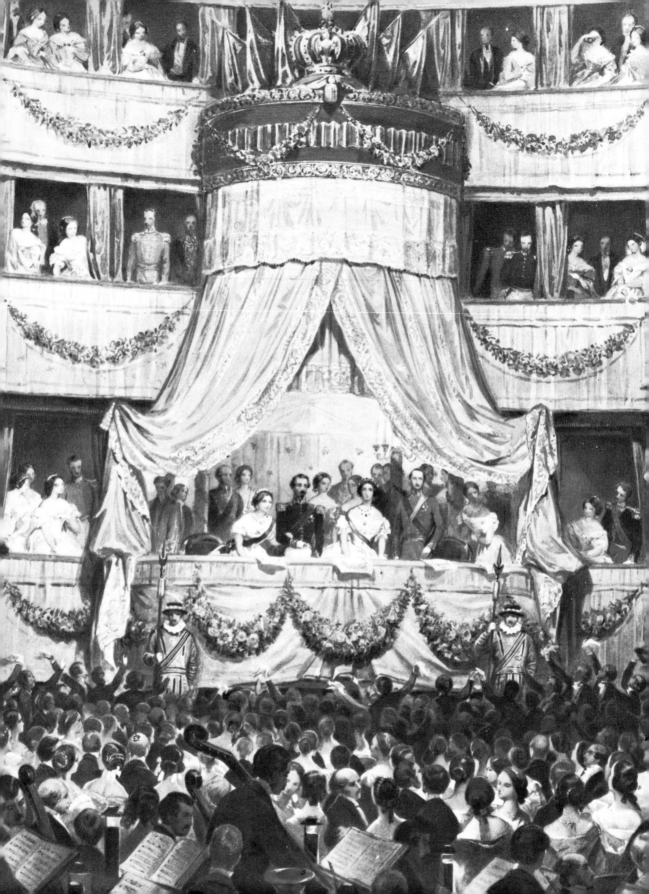

Queen Victoria, Prince Albert, the Emperor Napoleon III and the Empress Eugénie at a performance of 'Fidelio' at the Italian Opera, Covent Garden, 19 April 1855. Watercolour by Louis Haghe. Reproduced by gracious permission of Her Majesty The Queen.

Wales. This visit marked his own acceptance as a European sovereign.

Napoleon I had planned to launch his invasion of England from Boulogne; now, on 18 August 1855, his nephew waited there to greet the Prince Regent's niece. As Prince Albert observed: 'Whilst our fleet saluted us from the very anchorage which Nelson traversed for the purpose of preventing the invasion, many of the French regimental bands played *Rule Britannia!* in reply. So numerous were the strange impressions wrought by the contrast of past with present, that one could often only wonder.'

The royal yacht had been timed to enter the harbour at one o'clock, but it was nearly two o'clock before it anchored, and salvos were fired from the surrounding forts. The Emperor crossed the gangway, which was draped in purple velvet, and kissed Queen Victoria's hand. Then he led her ashore, Prince Albert and the children following. Napoleon III appeared to his best advantage on horseback; and, when his guests were settled in their barouche, he rode beside them to the railway station. It was dark when the royal and imperial train reached Paris. A deputation from the National Guard presented a bouquet to the Queen as she alighted at the Gare du Nord.

She and her family were to stay at the now-vanished palace of Saint-Cloud. Albert Vandam, the author of *An Englishman in Paris*, recalled: 'By a very delicate attention, the private apartments of the Queen had, in many ways, been made to look as much as possible like those at Windsor Castle. . . . In addition to this, the most valuable pictures had been borrowed from the Louvre to enhance the splendour of the reception and dining-rooms, while none but crack regiments in full dress were told off for duty.' Other arrangements were less fortunate. Lady Augusta Bruce learned that the maids 'did not seem to know their business as ours do, for instance [at dinner] you constantly heard behind your chair a great scuffle of five or six over something, and an authoritative "Imbécile!"' This 'seemed to denote that all was not going on precisely as smoothly as could be wished.'

France had followed England's example. This summer there was an International Exhibition in Paris. On 20 August Queen Victoria visited the Fine Arts section; then she drove to several points of interest in Paris, and along the eastern end of the rue de

Rivoli, which Baron Haussmann had recently completed. Paris, wrote Prince Albert,

> is signally beautified by the rue de Rivoli, the boulevard de Strasbourg, the completion of the Louvre, . . . and especially by the laying out of the ornamental grounds in the Bois de Boulogne, which really may be said to vie with the finest English parks. How all this could have been done in so short a time no one comprehends. On the other hand, a painful impression was produced by Neuilly [where Louis-Philippe had lived], now laid in ruins, with grass growing over them, and by the chapel of St Ferdinand, with the beautiful monument to the Duke of Orleans. Both of these spots we visited with the Emperor. Strange! No less remarkable than that, after the great review, we went down in our uniforms, by torchlight (for it was now dark) with him and Prince Napoleon into the tomb of Napoleon, while the organ of the Church of the Invalides played *God Save the Queen.* . . .

There were more frivolous moments. The Comédie-Française came to Saint-Cloud to perform *Les Demoiselles de Saint-Cyr.* The Queen had already seen the play in London, and enjoyed it so much that she had asked to see it again. A few days later, Albert Vandam met Dumas in the street. 'Well, you ought to be pleased', he said. 'Not only has the Queen asked to see your piece, . . . but she even enjoyed it much better the second time.' 'Just like its author', Dumas answered. 'The more you know him, the more you like him. But I know what she would have enjoyed even more than seeing my play, and that would have been seeing me. . . . Such a remarkable woman, who will probably become the greatest woman of the century, should have met the greatest man in France, . . . Alexander, King of the Romantic World.'

On 21 August the Queen went to Versailles, and attended a gala performance at the Opéra. After a concert and a ballet, the curtain rose on a backdrop of the Tower of London; and, as it did so, reported Mme Baroche, the politician's wife, the stars of the Opéra 'sang *God Save the Queen* with such purity and power that it seemed like a revelation of that noble air'. The Duchesse de Dino, a waspish socialite, noted in her diary that 'Prince Albert strictly obeyed the rules of marriage; for, seated between the Empress Eugénie, who was wonderfully beautiful, and Princess Mathilde, who has notable attractions, he hardly addressed a word to either of them.'

Visit of Napoleon III and the Empress Eugénie with Queen Victoria and Prince Albert to the Crystal Palace, Sydenham, 20 April 1855. Photograph by P. H. Delamotte. Reproduced by gracious permission of Her Majesty The Queen.

State visit of Queen Victoria and Prince Albert to France. Their entry into Paris with Napoleon III and the Empress Eugénie, 18 August 1855. Watercolour by E. Gudrard. Reproduced by gracious permission of Her Majesty The Queen.

Next day the Queen paid a second visit to the Exhibition. On the 23rd she spent several hours at the Louvre, and attended the ball which was given in her honour by the Municipality of Paris.

> I shall not attempt to describe that entertainment [wrote Vandam], the decorations and flowers of which alone cost three hundred and fifty thousand francs. The whole had been arranged under the superintendence of Baltard, the architect of the Halles Centrales. But I remember one little incident which caused a flutter of surprise among the Court ladies. . . . The royal matron of thirty-five, with a goodly family growing up around her, executed every step as her dancing master had taught her, and with none of the listlessness that was supposed to be the 'correct thing'. I was standing close to [Marshal] Canrobert, who had been recalled to resume his functions near the Emperor. After watching the Queen for a minute or so, he turned to the lady on his arm. 'By God, she dances like her soldiers fight, correct to the end.'

On 24 August the Queen paid a third visit to the Exhibition; soon after the carriages had passed down the Champs-Élysées, Vandam encountered the poet Béranger.

> The old man seemed in a great hurry, which was rather surprising, because he rarely put himself out for anything. I asked him the reason of his haste. 'I want to see your queen', he replied. . . .
>
> 'I thought you did not trouble yourself much about royalty', I remarked. 'You refused to go and see the Empress, and you rush along to see the Queen?'
>
> 'No; I am going to see the woman. If there were many women like her, I should forgive them for being queens.'
>
> Her Majesty never heard of this. It was the most magnificent and, at the same time, most witty tribute to her private virtues.

And so the wonderful week continued. On 25 August it ended with a ball at Versailles. The Empress was pregnant, and could not attend most of the events, but she had presided over the transformation of the Galerie des Glaces. This had been inspired by a print of some festive royal occasion in the days of Louis XV. Garlands of roses hung between the forty chandeliers, and the gallery was lit by at least three hundred thousand candles. There was another blaze of glory. At the stroke of ten the gardens at Versailles 'became all of a sudden ablaze with rockets and Chinese candles; it was the beginning of the fireworks, the principal piece of which represented Windsor Castle'.

Two days later, the Queen left for home. 'She feels the cordiality immensely,' wrote Lady Augusta, 'and the idea of cementing a lasting union is, I see, one which kindles her enthusiasm and delights her. Then I think she is *quite* charmed with the Emperor.'

The new Balmoral Castle was occupied for the first time this September. Three days after the Queen's arrival came long-awaited news. After months of siege, Sebastopol had fallen to the allies.

> God be praised for it [wrote the Queen]! Our delight was great. Albert said they should go at once and light the bonfire which had been prepared when the false report of the fall of the town had arrived last year. In a few minutes, Albert and all the gentlemen, in every species of attire, sallied forth, followed by all the servants, and gradually by all the population of the village – keepers, gillies, workmen – up to the top of the cairn. We waited, and saw them light the bonfire; accompanied by general cheering. It blazed forth brilliantly, and we could see the numerous figures surrounding it – some dancing, all shouting; Ross playing his pipes, and Grant and Macdonald firing off guns continually. The whole house seemed in a wonderful state of excitement. The boys were with difficulty awakened, and when at last this was the case, they begged leave to go up to the top of the cairn. We remained till a quarter to twelve; and, just as I was undressing, all the people came down under the windows, the pipes playing, the people singing, firing off guns, and cheering . . . .

Fresh excitement followed. The Queen had invited Prince Frederick William of Prussia to Balmoral; and, though he was only twenty-three, and the Princess Royal was not yet fifteen, he asked the Queen's permission to propose to her.

> September 29, 1855 [recorded the Queen in her diary]. Our dear Victoria was this day engaged to Prince Frederick William of Prussia, who had been on a visit to us since the 14th. He had already spoken to us of his wishes; but we were uncertain, on account of her extreme youth, whether he should speak to her himself, or wait till he came back again. However, we felt it was better he should do so; and during our ride up Craig-na-Ban this afternoon, he picked a piece of white heather, the emblem of good luck, which he gave to her; and this enabled him to make an allusion to his hopes and wishes.

For the Queen and her husband, this was a happy conclusion to their own well-laid plans. Prince Albert remained an ardent German. Now, in the course of time, his favourite child would be Queen of Prussia. If, as he hoped, Prussia united Germany under her, Vicky would be Empress of Germany. But, as the Duke of Saxe-Coburg explained, she was not to make a purely political alliance. 'My brother loved his eldest daughter far too much and too tenderly to place political views decisively foremost. . . . For many years it had been his wish, as I had often observed, to behold in high position this, his favourite child, in whose education he had taken the largest personal share. With paternal delight he thought of his promising, highly-gifted, early-ripening daughter on a powerful throne, but I well knew that, above all things, he wished her to be happy.'

Englishmen did not share the Prince's Prussian aspirations. They had long been tired of German influence on the English throne. No doubt they also felt that the Princess Royal was too young to think of marriage. When her engagement was announced, it was far from popular.

The Royal Family at Balmoral, 29 September 1855, the day of the Princess Royal's engagement to Prince Frederick William of Prussia. L. to R.: Prince Alfred, Prince Frederick William of Prussia, Princess Alice, the Prince of Wales, Queen Victoria, Prince Albert, the Princess Royal. Photograph by George Washington Wilson. Reproduced by gracious permission of Her Majesty The Queen.

For some time Prince Albert had been highly critical of the British Diplomatic Service. Talking to Lady Augusta Bruce at dinner, he had lamented 'that men are not brought on and trained as in any other profession'. Besides, he had added, British diplomats did not attempt to improve their opportunities, 'and our diplomacy is consequently the worst. They know, generally speaking, nothing of the countries and the people among whom they live. . . .' Now, back at Windsor, in October 1855, he finished a memorandum on examinations and new rules of admission to the Diplomatic Service. He also prepared an address on the influence of science and art on industry; he was to deliver it when he laid the foundation stone of the Birmingham and Midland Counties Institute. He had 'a superabundance of business'.

Besides, the end of the Crimean War was in sight, and the Queen was much concerned about the honours which she should bestow. For men of conspicuous valour, officers and privates alike, she instituted the Victoria Cross. As a decoration she ranked it above all that she could confer. The cross itself was to be made of iron from the cannon taken at Sebastopol. Prince Albert had conceived the idea of the decoration; Prince Albert designed the cross, and no doubt Prince Albert decided on the motto. If they chose the motto 'For the Brave', it would imply that only those who had earned the Victoria Cross were considered brave. They therefore chose the motto 'For Valour'.

To Miss Nightingale, who had transformed the army medical service, and organized the hospital at Scutari, the Queen sent a letter in her own hand, and a brooch which her husband had designed. It bore her crown and cypher and a St George's Cross in red enamel with the inscription: 'Blessed are the Merciful.' Miss Nightingale was received at Balmoral by her Sovereign.

> She is much less altered than expected [wrote Lady Augusta] – her beautiful countenance looks to me more beautiful than ever. – Her hair is short and she wears a little plain morning cap – her black gown high, open in front. The Queen and children delighted with her. . . . She is so modest and retiring and fearful of notice – but when people require information and are anxious to discuss with her for useful purposes, then, in her firm, gentle way, she speaks with a lucidity and clearness quite as extraordinary as any other of her remarkable gifts. . . .

It was delightful to see her [at Balmoral], and how the Queen and Prince listened to and spoke with her – the Queen shewed her a whole book of photographs she has had done of the wounded and the most distinguished soldiers, with a notice of each, *little* required by the royal memory !! . .

[Miss N.] wears the Queen's brooch which her soldiers are so proud of, taking it as a *personal compliment* to each individual!

On 30 March 1856, the Peace of Paris was signed at the Tuileries. Further honours followed. The Queen offered Palmerston the Garter as a tribute to the manner in which he had maintained the honour and interests of the country. Lord Palmerston proved himself for once perfectly correct. His task, he replied, had been 'rendered comparatively easy by the enlightened views which Your Majesty has taken of all the great affairs in which Your Majesty's Empire has been engaged'.

The Queen then turned, once again, to an honour which she felt had been better earned than any: an honour which was long overdue. In a substantial memorandum she set out her case for conferring on her husband and on 'all future Consorts of Queens' the title of Prince Consort and precedence by law next to the Sovereign. She circulated her memorandum to Lord Derby and Lord Palmerston, and the Lord Chancellor drafted a Bill to remedy this 'strange anomaly'. Lord Derby thought that if 'The Prince Consort Bill' were brought before the House of Commons, it might be postponed and criticized in a painful manner. The Queen took his advice, and abandoned the idea of making his new title the subject of a vote in Parliament.

She was wise to do so. She had now been married for sixteen years, and her husband's achievement was evident. People who met him or worked with him respected his character and his intelligence, his immense ability and his gift for organization. But these are not endearing qualities. In spite of his years of labour for the general good, even despite the Great Exhibition, he remained unloved and mistrusted. Indeed, in 1854, an anonymous pamphleteer had felt obliged to come to his defence in *Observations on the Character and Conduct of the Prince Consort* [sic], *in reference to the aspersions on His Royal Highness.*

There are [wrote the pamphleteer] three subjects which for some years past have occupied a prominent place in public consideration –

Prince Albert 1855. Photograph by J. E. Mayall. Reproduced by gracious permission of Her Majesty The Queen.

the education of the humbler orders – the improvement of their
dwellings – and the advancement of agriculture. The Prince has made
himself the patron of them all. . . . If we do not find his name
prominent among the political clubs, the winners and losers at
Newmarket, or in the easy dissipations of fashionable life, we find it
in the meetings for popular instruction, for the building of model
lodging-houses, for founding dockyards, excavating canals, and
ennobling agriculture into a national science. . . .

The achievement remained, and it increased; and yet, two years
later, another pamphlet appeared: *Prince Albert. Why is he unpopular?*

> In this world of contradiction there is [declared the author] one fact
> that no one can be found to contravert, and that is the unpopularity of
> His Royal Highness Prince Albert.
> It is a feeling that, commencing with his advent to this country
> twenty *[sic]* years ago, has been steadily gaining ground . . . with his
> continued residence. Although a feeling shared by almost everyone,
> no one can give a rational cause for its existence. There is no use in
> shirking the question. . . . There is the stern, incontrovertible fact,
> that Prince Albert, the consort, during nearly a quarter of a century
> *[sic]*, of the most amiable and beloved Sovereign that has ever sat on
> the throne of these seagirt isles, is the most unpopular man in them.

In this summer of 1856 Lord Hardinge had a paralytic stroke,
and resigned as Commander-in-Chief. Once again, the post had
to be filled. It would never have done to suggest Prince Albert
again. No Government could have carried through so unpopular
an appointment. But the Queen wanted to give the post to one of
the Family. She nominated her cousin, George, Duke of Cambridge. He held the office for thirty-nine years, and refused every
suggestion of reform. Her personal influence had to be exercised
once more in order to ensure his retirement.

Meanwhile, in July, in summer sunshine, the Queen welcomed home the Guards on their return from the Crimea. From
the balcony of Buckingham Palace she saw them march past, as
she had seen them leave on a cold February morning more than
two years before.

The Queen's ninth and youngest child, Princess Beatrice, was
born on 14 April 1857. 'Mother and baby are well', reported

Prince Albert to Princess Augusta of Prussia, the future mother-in-law of the Princess Royal. 'Baby practises her scales like a good *prima-donna* before a performance, and has a good voice! Victoria counts the hours and minutes like a prisoner.'

It was now time to correct, once and for all, the anomaly that caused her such humiliation. She ran no risks in Parliament. On 25 June, by Royal Letters Patent, which nobody could challenge, she conferred on her husband the title of Prince Consort of the United Kingdom of Great Britain and Ireland. *The Times* devoted a leading article to the event. 'In spite of the poet', the leader ended, 'there is much in a name, and if there be increased homage rendered to the new title on the banks of the Spree and the Danube, the English people will be happy to sanction and adopt it.' 'I now present myself before you as an entire stranger, *Prince Consort,* to wit.' So wrote the Prince himself to his step-mother. 'Now I have a legal status in the English hierarchy.' Ironically, he did not appreciate Queen Victoria's gesture. It ought, he felt, to have been made on his marriage.

> The nation [he had explained to Stockmar, not so long ago], the nation, slow of thought and uneducated, has never given itself the trouble to consider what really is the position of the husband of a Queen Regnant. When I first came over here, I was met by this want of knowledge and unwillingness to give a thought to the position of this luckless personage. Peel cut down my income, Wellington refused me my rank, the Royal Family cried out against the foreign interloper, the Whigs in office were only inclined to concede to me just as much space as I could stand upon. The Constitution is silent as to the Consort of the Queen; – even Blackstone ignores him, and yet there he was, and not to be done without. . . .

Now he had toiled for seventeen years. The honour, such as it was, had come too late, and even now it was no national recognition of his services. As the Queen was one day to observe: 'You cannot force people here to be enthusiastic if they don't choose.'

Yet again the Prince Consort turned to his despatches and memoranda. There was grave trouble in India. It was now a century since Clive's victory at Plassey, but the native forces in India were still very large in comparison with the European. There had recently been signs of insubordination. The Bengal troops had been issued with cartridges which were said to be greased with the fat of pigs and cows. The use of this was abhorrent, on religious grounds, to Hindus and Muslims. The Governor-General of Bengal assured the Sepoys that no offence or injury was intended to their caste; but on 10 May there had been a mutiny among the garrison at Meerut. Now, at the end of June, it had spread to twenty-two stations.

Six months ago, the Prince had warned the Government that they did not have enough reserves of men or material, and now India was wanting both, and there were scarcely enough in England for home defence, should an emergency arise. During the summer, he drafted a series of strong notes for the Queen to send to Palmerston. 'Ten Battalions of Militia to be called out is quite inadequate; forty, at least, ought to be the number, for these also exist only on paper. The augmentation of Cavalry and the Guards has not yet been ordered. Financial difficulties don't exist; . . . and this appears hardly the moment to make savings on the Army estimates.' The note was despatched from Osborne on 22 August, and it was answered by Palmerston that day. Another note was sent at once: 'The Queen hopes the Cabinet will yet look the whole question in the face.'

The Prince's forebodings about India proved to be justified. Large reinforcements were sent from England. Lucknow was besieged. The Queen's autumn visit to Balmoral was darkened by the news of the massacre of the English women and children at Cawnpore, after the surrender of the fort, and the perilous position of the Lucknow garrison. Finally Lucknow was re-lieved, the Mutiny was suppressed, and the first steps were taken to simplify government in India, by bringing the country under the sole and direct power of the Crown.

7

The Last Years of
The Prince Consort

A momentous marriage was soon to take place: the marriage of the Princess Royal to Prince Frederick William of Prussia.

In December 1857 the Queen sent Lady Canning her thoughts.

> Our poor Victoria is wretchedly low at taking leave of *all* she loves & cares for – & of every fête & anniversary being the *last* she shall spend here as a happy innocent Child! She feels that she leaves a *very very* happy Home & I am sure she will feel *very* sad & lonely at first – tho' she is excessively attached to Prince Frederic & he to her. On the 25th January the Marriage takes place & on the 2nd February she is to leave her happy Home!

So happy, indeed, that the prospect of the marriage seemed like the prospect of a funeral. The Queen confessed later to her daughter: 'Yes, dearest, it is an awful moment to have to give one's innocent child up to a man, be he ever so kind and good – and to think of all that she must go through – (indeed I have not got over it yet) and that last night when we took you to your room, and you cried so much, I said to Papa as we came back "after all, it is like taking a poor lamb to be sacrificed."'

The marriage also brought with it problems of precedence. As the Queen explained to Vicky, she must always distinguish between her conduct to Prussian royalty and to 'the Russian family who have never been considered as better or as high as our family. . . . These are things which may appear trifles, but which the honour and dignity of one's country do not allow to be overlooked.' Some had been rash enough to suggest that, since the bridegroom was a Prussian Prince, the marriage should take place in Berlin. Queen Victoria did not argue with people, she

Queen Victoria, the Prince Co[nsort]
and the Princess Royal before t[he]
Princess's marriage, 25 January
1858. Daguerreotype by T. R.
Williams. Reproduced by grac[ious]
permission of Her Majesty Th[e]
Queen.

informed them. She informed her Foreign Secretary: 'Whatever may be the usual practice of Prussian princes, it is not *every* day that one marries the eldest daughter of the Queen of England. The question therefore must be considered as settled and closed.'

The marriage took place in the Chapel Royal, St James's Palace, and the reception at Buckingham Palace. The wedding cake was six feet high. When it was cut, the Prince Consort retired to his desk to tell Stockmar: 'All went well. The young people are now changing their dresses, and start in half an hour for Windsor; we are just going over to them. God's blessing be upon them!'

The 'Honey Couple', as the Queen called them, set out for their brief honeymoon. On 2 February, in the royal yacht, they sailed from Gravesend for Antwerp, on their way to Berlin.

Rarely, one feels, had a marriage brought such lamentations.

> Once more [wrote the bride that day to her mother], once more before this dreadful day ends, let your child thank you for all your kindness – for all your love. Once more let me repeat that dreadful word goodbye, which twice today had well-nigh broke my heart.
>
> Nobody knows what I suffered today as we went down the staircase at dear Buckingham Palace with an aching head and a far more aching heart – and hardest of all almost the last farewell here on board.

The last farewell had been for the Prince Consort. His eldest daughter adored him; he himself was desolate at the departure of his favourite child. 'I am not of a demonstrative nature', he confessed to her, 'and therefore you can hardly know how dear you have always been to me, and what a void you have left behind in my heart; yet not in my heart, for there assuredly you will abide henceforth, as till now you have done, but in my daily life, which is evermore reminding my heart of your absence.' The letter, from father to daughter, was a letter of love; it has an urgency and conviction lacking in his letters to his wife.

The Queen herself deeply missed her daughter. There was, however, one consolation. Now – perhaps for the first time – she found a woman in whom she could confide her most intimate thoughts. 'There is', she wrote, 'no longer anything between us which I cannot touch with you – and a married daughter, be she

The marriage of the Princess Royal and Prince Frederick William of Prussia in the Chapel Royal, St James's Palace, 25 January 1858. L. to R.: Prince William and Princess Augusta of Prussia, the Archbishop of Canterbury, Prince Frederick William, the Princess Royal; to the right of the bridesmaids Prince Alfred, behind him the Prince Consort and King Leopold, the Prince of Wales, Queen Victoria with Prince Arthur and Prince Leopold, the Princesses Louise, Helena and Alice, and behind them the Duchess of Kent and Lord Palmerston with the Sword of State. Painting by John Phillip. Copyright reserved.

ever so young, is at once on a par with her mother.' And so Queen Victoria began the voluminous correspondence which continued for the rest of her long life.

She wrote as she certainly must have talked: with common sense, some naïvety, much shrewdness, and a vehemence which occasionally led her into indiscretion. She was immensely affectionate, she was extremely domestic; and she was so royal that, reading her correspondence, one often feels one ought to drop a curtsey. All Queen Victoria's qualities glow in these letters to her eldest daughter.

She shows herself a devoted mother, interested in every detail of her children's lives ('air, air is what you want, and not hot stuffy rooms and theatres, or you will become sickly and old before you are 20!'). She revels in Princess Beatrice, less than a year old, wearing little silk stockings and pink satin shoes; she waits, all anxiety, for the engagement of the gentle, self-effacing Princess Alice. She is constantly concerned about Prince Leopold's health ('he bruises as much as ever but *unberufen* 1000 times – is free from any at present'). She perpetually delights in Prince Alfred ('always so great a favourite, with his dear, handsome good face – and so like dear Papa'). She worries, of course, continually about the Prince of Wales. 'The systematic idleness, laziness – disregard of everything is enough to break one's heart, and fills me with indignation. . . . To you I own, I am wretched about it. But don't mention this to a human being!'

General Grey, wrote Lady Augusta Bruce, 'says he has been enchanted with the Prince of Wales, he is such a fine, nice Boy, and behaves so well'. Alas, the Prince of Wales could not do right in his mother's eyes. By some unhappy tradition, the kings of the House of Hanover had always detested their eldest sons; and Queen Victoria could rarely bring herself to show sympathy or affection for her heir. His birth had given her far more pain than any other birth; his looks were constantly deplored (his Coburg nose, his 'very large lips', his hair style, his knock knees, his want of chin). He was – said his mother – lazy, ignorant and dull. 'He is my caricature, that is the misfortune', she burst out in a moment of confidence.('Only one thing pains me, when I think of it', Princess Frederick William confessed, 'and that is the relation between you and Bertie.') 'Oh! dear,' writes the Queen in 1859, 'what would happen if I were to die next winter! One shudders to

The Princess Royal and Prince Frederick William on their honeymoon at Windsor Castle, 29 January 1858. Photograph by Bambridge. Reproduced by gracious permission of Her Majesty The Queen.

think of it. . . . The greatest improvement I fear will never make him fit for his position. His only safety and the country's – is his implicit reliance, in every thing, on dearest Papa, that perfection of human beings!'

Yet, to her eldest daughter – and, perhaps, to her alone – the Queen confessed that her husband had his imperfections. He was something of a misogynist. 'That despising of our poor degraded sex', the Queen wrote to her daughter, '. . . is a little in all clever men's natures; dear Papa even is not quite exempt though he would not admit it – but he laughs and sneers constantly at many of them.' He clearly felt that they deserved little attention. He dictated his children's lives – at times without reference to the Queen's own wishes. He sent Prince Alfred away to sea when he was fourteen, and she thought him too young. 'I have been shamefully deceived about Affie', she complained to her daughter. 'It was promised me that the last year before he went to sea, he should be with us, instead of which he was taken away and I saw but very little of him, and now he is to go away for many months and I shall not see him [till] God knows! when, and Papa is most cruel upon the subject.' The Prince snubbed his wife 'several times very sharply' for writing often to her daughter, and for making her write in return. He insisted on the Queen's leaving Osborne for London 'for no earthly reason but that tiresome horticultural garden – which', said the Queen, 'I curse for more reasons than one'. She was distraught to have to leave 'poor little, sick Leopold behind here – in his bed which makes me sadly anxious, and adds to my low spirits! They say there is no danger at present, but I own I think it both cruel and wrong to leave a sick child behind. . . . I am very much annoyed and distressed at being forced to leave him by the very person who ought to wish me to stay. But men have not the sympathy and anxiety of women. Oh! no!' It seems extraordinary that the Queen did not insist on staying with her child; but, indignant though she was, she submitted to the Prince. The superbly independent girl had become an all too docile woman.

The Prince made his wife feel intellectually inferior, and, indeed, he made her feel inferior as a human being. 'We poor creatures', the Queen lamented, 'are born for man's pleasure and amusement.' And again: 'All marriage is such a lottery – the happiness is always an exchange – though it may be a very happy

Queen Victoria and the Prince Consort, c. 1858. Reproduced by gracious permission of Her Majesty The Queen.

one – still the poor woman is bodily and morally the husband's slave.' And yet again: 'Men are very selfish and the woman's devotion is always one of submission which makes our poor sex very unenviable.' And again: 'I know that God has willed it so and that these are the trials which we poor women must go through; no father, no man can feel this! Papa never would enter into it all! As in fact he seldom can in my very violent feelings.' There, indeed, was a devastating comment on the marriage.

The Prince Consort had not, it seems, sympathized with his wife in the trials of pregnancy and childbirth. He had never felt estatic about his own children when they were small (though 'after a certain age, if they are nice (and not like Bertie and Leopold were) he is very fond of playing with them)'. He was, however, concerned about their intellectual formation. He readily talked politics and military matters over breakfast, and he summoned his children, in turn, at six o'clock in the evening, for improving conversation. Marriage, one suspects, had made him arrogant, domineering and selfish. He had always worried about his health, and now he was plunged into despondency by a bout of toothache. 'Dear Papa', wrote the Queen, 'never allows he is any better or will try to get over it, but makes such a miserable face that people always think he's very ill. . . . His nervous system is easily excited and irritated, and he's so completely overpowered by everything.' Reading the Queen's correspondence with her daughter, and reading especially between the lines, one becomes aware of an autocratic Consort, demanding sole control of his wife and family, sole control of English politics, and unremitting, undivided sympathy.

And yet – at least to outward eyes – the marriage remained exemplary; and the Queen remained extremely happy. Early in February 1858, within a few days of her daughter's wedding, there came the eighteenth anniversary of the Queen's own marriage. 'It has brought', she wrote, 'such universal blessings on this country and Europe. For what has not my beloved and perfect Albert done? Raised monarchy to the *highest* pinnacle of *respect*, and rendered it *popular* beyond what it *ever* was in this country!' In spite of the hyperbole, there was some truth in the statement. The Prince himself could never be popular; but their life together had erased the memory of the Georges, and immensely strengthened the Throne. And, in a letter to her eldest daughter, the Queen herself explained the extraordinary intensity of her relationship with her husband.

> I cannot ever think or admit [she wrote with a certain want of tact] that anyone can be as blessed as I am with such a husband and such a perfection as a husband; for Papa has been and is everything to me. I had led a very unhappy life as a child – had no scope for my very violent feelings of affection – had no brothers and sisters to live with – never had had a father – from my unfortunate circumstances was not on a comfortable or at all intimate or confidential footing with my mother (so different from you to me) much as I love her now – and did not know what a happy domestic life was! All this is the complete contrast to your happy childhood and home. Consequently I owe everything to dearest Papa. He was my father, my protector, my guide and adviser in all and everything, my mother (I might almost say) as well as my husband. I suppose no one ever was so completely altered and changed in every way as I was by dearest Papa's blessed influence. Papa's position towards me is therefore of a very peculiar character and when he is away I feel quite paralysed.

It was perhaps the most revealing passage in Queen Victoria's massive correspondence.

On 27 May 1858 the Prince Consort set out for Coburg. He picked pansies for his wife at the Rosenau, and sent her cowslips, with the injunction: 'Make tea of them, in honour of me, and let Bertie have some.' On 4 June, at Babelsberg, he was with his daughter, and reported: 'The relation between the young people is all that can be desired.' Vicky was now pregnant; and on 23 June, from Buckingham Palace, he wrote to her: 'I suppose I may now assume that I have every chance of becoming at 39 a venerable grandpapa. This will give to the coming grey hairs in my whiskers a certain significance, which they have hitherto lacked.'

We may look at him, now through the eyes of a contemporary, the anonymous editor of his speeches.

> The Prince had a noble presence. His carriage was erect: his figure betokened strength and activity; and his demeanour was dignified. He had a staid, earnest, thoughtful look when he was in a grave mood; but when he smiled . . . his whole countenance was irradiated with pleasure; and there was a pleasant sound and a heartiness about

his laugh which will not soon be forgotten by those who were wont to hear it.

He was very handsome as a young man; but . . . his countenance never assumed a nobler aspect, nor had more real beauty in it, than in the last year or two of his life.

There was beauty, and there was increasing sadness.

July 1858 was one of the warmest Julys ever known in England; the condition of the Thames threatened to drive Parliament from Westminster. After a month's stay at Osborne, on their private beach and their green estates, the Queen and her husband, with the Prince of Wales, paid a state visit to Napoleon III and the Empress Eugénie at Cherbourg.

The Anglo-French alliance was considerably less strong than it had been in the Crimean War, and England looked on France with her customary suspicion. On 2 August, two days before she was due to arrive in France, the Queen sent an urgent note to the Prime Minister, on the subject of French naval preparations. The reports which had been received disclosed 'a state of things of the greatest moment to this country. It will be the first time in her history', wrote the Queen, 'that she will find herself in an absolute minority of ships on the sea. . . . The Queen thinks it irreconcilable with the duty which the Government owes to the country to be aware of this state of things without straining every nerve to remedy it.'

Two days later, the Queen and her husband sailed into Cherbourg.

The great fort was nearly completed [Sarah Tytler wrote], and the harbour was full of French war-vessels as Her Majesty steamed in, on the evening of the 4th August, receiving such a salute from the ships and the fortress itself as seemed to shake earth and sky. The Emperor and Empress, who arrived the same day, came on board at eight o'clock, and were cordially received by the Queen and the Prince, though the relations between England and France were not quite so assured as when their soldiers were brothers-in-arms in the Crimea. After the visitors left, the Queen's journal records that she went below and read, and nearly finished, 'that most interesting book *Jane Eyre*'.

Next evening a State dinner was held on board the *Bretagne*.

The speechmaking, to which one may say all Europe was listening, was [continued the biographer] a trying experience. The Emperor, though he changed colour, spoke well 'in a powerful voice', proposing the health of the Queen, the Prince, and the Royal Family, and declaring his adherence to the French alliance with England. The Prince replied. 'He did it very well, though he hesitated once', the Queen reported. 'I sat shaking, with my eyes riveted to the table.' The duty done, a great relief was felt, as the speechmakers, with the Queen and the Empress, retired to the privacy of the cabin, shook hands, and compared notes on their nervousness.

The Prince – and not the Queen – had spoken as the Head of State. He had been so nervous that he suffered from a migraine next day.

He had also sent for the Ministers in attendance, and pointed out the strength of the Cherbourg fortifications. The royal salute itself had revealed it. The Prince considered that the new fort was a grave threat to England, and demanded immediate counter-measures. At the end of the visit, he said: 'I am conscious of a change in the Emperor', and he spoke of 'the enormous crimes which he is meditating against Europe'.

This sense of an impending onslaught by the French coloured the Prince's outlook on European affairs. He felt that the English Government was dangerously lax about re-armament, and, as he wrote to Stockmar: 'We are constantly digging our spurs into their sides.' Richard Cobden dismissed the Prince's 'rifle mania' as 'pure Germanism in the disguise of British patriotism'. He suggested that the Prince only wished to see England strong so that she could support the anti-French policy of Prussia. But the Prince was not apprehensive because of the danger to Prussia. He felt that the Emperor was toying with the idea of European war. 'I really *hope* that there is no *real* desire for war in the Emperor's mind', the Queen wrote to the King of the Belgians. 'We have also explained to him strongly how *entirely* he would *alienate* us from him if there was any *attempt to disturb standing and binding treaties.*'

In February 1858 there had been political change. Lord Palmerston's Government had fallen; and the task of reorganization in India had been assumed by Lord Derby's Administration. On 1 November the Queen transferred the government of India from the East India Company to the sovereign. At the same time she appointed her Governor-General - Viscount Canning, Charlotte's husband - to be India's first Viceroy. 'If it was not for the heat and the insects,' she wrote to Charlotte, 'how much I should like to see India, that most luxuriant country full of such wealth & I am sure intended some day to become civilized.'

It was suggested that she should take the title of Empress of India, but the idea was not pursued until 1876; it was then revived by Disraeli. The Queen was exceedingly tenacious of royal prerogatives. She insisted that the Secretary of State for India should send her all despatches, and all the drafts of instructions or orders, in boxes marked 'For Approval'. She asked Lord Derby if he would draft the Proclamation for India 'in his excellent language, bearing in mind that it is a female sovereign who speaks to more than 100,000,000 of Eastern people on assuming the direct Government over them after a bloody civil war, giving them pledges which her future reign is to redeem. . . . Such a document should breathe feelings of generosity, benevolence, and religious feeling. . . .' The draft Proclamation was written as the Queen desired. She also decided to found a new Order of Chivalry, the Star of India, and among the first to receive it were to be the native princes who had remained loyal to the Crown. In these conciliatory counsels, in these farsighted observations, in the considered detail, even in the anxiety to preserve the royal prerogatives, one may discern the hand of the Prince Consort.

He laboured on, losing himself in work, yet always discontented. Nineteen years ago, at the time of his engagement, he had written to his stepmother: 'It is a support to one to feel that one has used all ones endeavours and strength in some great object, decisive for the welfare of so many.' He had used all his endeavours and strength, and he had received small thanks. His sense of British ingratitude seems even, for a moment, to have brought him into sympathy with the man who had long thwarted and ignored him. On 4 September, at Osborne, he wrote a memorandum on a 'most curious phenomenon': the unpopularity of Lord Palmerston. Suddenly, and for no apparent reason, the House of Commons had turned hostile to him.

It will hardly listen to him when he speaks. He is frequently received with hooting, and throughout the last Session it sufficed that

[he] took up any cause for the whole House to vote against it. . . .
How can this be accounted for? The man who was without rhyme or
reason stamped the only *English* statesman, the champion of liberty,
the man of the people, etc., etc., now, without his having changed in
any one respect, having still the same virtues and the same faults that
he always had, young and vigorous in his seventy-fifth year, and
having succeeded in his policy, is now considered the head of a
clique, the man of intrigue, past his work, etc., etc. – in fact hated!
and this throughout the country. . . .

Lord Palmerston himself remains, outwardly at least, quite cheerful, and seems to care very little about his reverses. . . .

Under the Prince's sympathy one detects a sense of the injustice
done to himself, and perhaps a sense of envy. Palmerston at
seventy-four was young and vigorous. He at thirty-nine was old
and tired. Palmerston was indifferent to unpopularity. The
Prince Consort was embittered by it.

No doubt on many subjects the Prince's judgment was at fault.
Yet everyone who talked to him was compelled to admire his
intellectual grasp. Lord Granville – who understood the working
of the Government machine – said of the Prince: 'His knowledge
and information were astonishing, and there is not a Department
of the Government regarding all the details and management of
which he is not much better informed and more capable than the
Minister at the head of it.'

It is sometimes said that if the Prince had lived there would
have been a clash between the Crown and the Cabinet. Admittedly he was determined that the Sovereign should not become,
in Stockmar's phrase, 'a mandarin figure, which has to nod its
head in assent, or shake it in denial, as its Minister pleases'. His
object was to increase the prestige and popularity of the Crown
by lifting it above political parties and by investing it with the
glamour of morality. The Prince was not aiming at absolutism:
instead, he saw the Sovereign as a partner with the Cabinet.

And so he worked on. In the morning he and the Queen were
called at seven by a wardrobe maid. The Prince got up almost at
once, put on a dressing-gown, and went straight to his sitting-
room where a green lamp – his 'little student's lamp' – was
already lighted on his desk. He generally worked with a fire of
which – except in winter – the Queen disapproved. During 'this

golden morning hour', as he called it, he wrote his letters and most of his drafts for the Queen. When he had dressed – he always wore the ribbon of the Garter under his waistcoat – he would have breakfast, during which he would read *The Times*. He would discuss with his secretaries the business of the day.

The Queen herself was disturbed by the unremitting, constant pressure on him. 'My greatest of all anxieties is that dearest Papa works too hard, wears himself quite out by all he does. It makes me often miserable. If it were not for Osborne and Balmoral and then again Windsor at Easter – I don't know what we should do.' Repeatedly in her letters we catch her anxiety about her husband's health. 'Poor dear Papa (who is very much fagged and has had toothache into the bargain) goes at 6 in the morning to Plymouth to open that great large bridge at Saltash over the Tamar and returns the same night at one!' 'Poor dear Papa had one of his stomach attacks on Monday, which made him look fearfully ill, but he remained on the field [at Aldershot] in that broiling sun the whole time. . . .' 'Dear Papa was a little indisposed with his old enemy, but it was not a very bad attack with sickness or shivering.'

The Prince was frequently unwell, and he was all too often melancholy.

> Your letter has found me in the enjoyment of the most glorious air, the most fragrant odours, the merriest choirs of birds and the most luxuriant verdure [so he wrote from Osborne to his eldest daughter]. And were there not so many things that reminded one of the so-called World (that is to say of miserable men) one might abandon oneself wholly to the enjoyment of the real world. There is no such good fortune, however, for poor me; and this being so one's feelings remain under the influence of the treadmill of never-ending business. The donkey in Carisbrooke, which you will remember, is my true counterpart. He, too, would rather munch thistles in the Castle Moat than turn round in the wheel at the Castle Well; and small are the thanks he gets for his labour.

The British had always considered the Prince Consort as a foreigner, and he himself had never lost the feeling of being an alien in an alien land. 'And it may be', as Charles Kingsley said, 'that he felt . . . that we were unjust to him; and that it bred in him a reserve, a shyness, which some took for pride, – though it was not pride, but a most noble modesty. . . .' The Queen adored him, and she still anticipated his every wish. But he longed for understanding and spiritual companionship, and these – for all her love – she could not give him. The Princess Royal, Princess Frederick William, had given him these things, and now he had had to let her go from him. His only real friends in England had been Anson and Peel, and both of them had died long ago. He was intensely lonely, and he was not strong enough to bear such loneliness. Since he was not really happy, he worked without remission.

As he grew older – aged still more by lack of sympathy, by the resentments he was forced to fight – his natural moodiness increased. 'The battle of life', explained his brother, 'rendered him more severe. . . . As he became more wrapped up in his own doctrines, he lost much of his natural cheerfulness.' He continued to labour for the good of mankind, but his misanthropy became more evident. He often said that he was tired of living.

Once he assured Lord Hardwicke: 'I have no wish for myself, and but one wish for the future, and that is, for the long life of the Queen.'

In November 1858 Stockmar had paid his last visit to England. Henceforth the old Baron no longer haunted the corridors of power – although his son, the young Baron, already hovered round Princess Frederick William, as her secretary. Figures from the past were departing. Figures of the future were about to make their appearances. 'I delight', the Queen told her daughter, 'in the idea of being a grandmama; to be that at 39 (D.V.) and to look and feel young is great fun, only I wish I could go through it for you, and save you all the annoyance.' The Prince Consort was exhausted; the Queen – only three months older – remained buoyant and vital, with a Hanoverian love of life.

On 27 January 1859, Victoria and Albert learned of the birth of their first grandchild. Princess Frederick William had had a painful labour. Her son, the future Kaiser, was born with a withered arm: a physical defect which was to warp his character, and so to help determine the future of Europe.

Meanwhile, in 1859, the peace of the Continent was broken when Austria declared war on Sardinia. With the help of Napoleon III, Victor Emmanuel regained the province of Lombardy, and began to consolidate Italy. Napoleon III had lost his old fascination for the Queen, and she began to think him more dangerous than fascinating. There had been fears that Prussia might join Austria, and she had urged him to do his utmost to localize the conflict, but he did little more than thank his Sister, warmly, for her advice. 'I am sick of all this horrid business', the Queen wrote to Princess Frederick William, 'of politics and Europe in general, and think you will hear some day of my going with the children to live in Australia'.

However, peace came in July, and she returned, as usual, to Osborne. 'Living here, and sitting out writing under the trees, as I am doing the whole morning – is most luxurious and enjoyable and I feel it is quite paradise.' Paradise it seemed to be. On 14 August Lady Augusta Bruce spent the afternoon at the Swiss Cottage 'with the Babes. Pr. Leopold in his little carriage with his arm round Baby [Princess Beatrice], every moment bending down to *hug her*. She is delicious – jabbers so fast and so plain, is

Princess Beatrice taking her first ride at Osborne on her second birthday, 14 April 1859. Photograph by Caldesi. Reproduced by gracious permission of Her Majesty The Queen.

full of wit and fun, and graceful as a fairy – meddles with everything, makes her remarks on all – quite exquisite.' Princess Beatrice seems, indeed, to have been a bewitching child.

The Queen says 'Baby mustn't have that, it's not good for Baby!'
'But she likes it, my dear', is her reply as she helps herself!
She adores her Mama, kisses her hand, is very grateful for the affection shewn her by her parents. She comes to the Duchess [of Kent] to be played to, and *sings the tunes* she wishes to have – quite correctly with a most huskey pot-house voice. I never [wrote Lady Augusta] heard anything like it. . . .

On the last day of August the Queen and her husband found themselves once more at Balmoral. On their way north, at Edinburgh, the Prince Consort had had a conference

with all the persons who are taking part in the education of the Prince of Wales. They all speak highly of him [this to Stockmar], and he seems to have shown zeal and goodwill. Dr Lyon Playfair is giving him lectures on chemistry in relation to manufactures, and at the

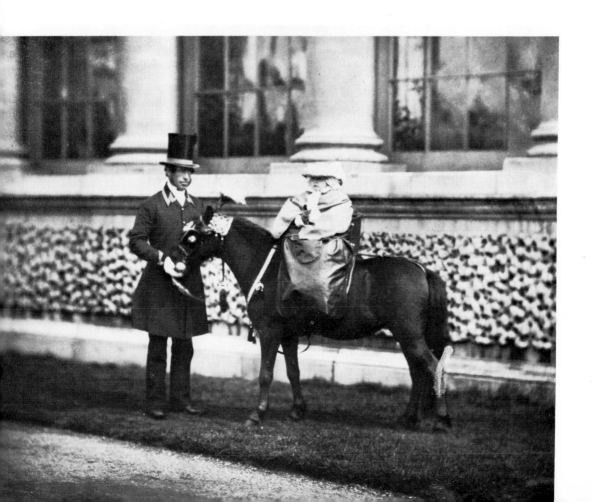

close of each special course he visits the appropriate manufactory with him, so as to explain its practical application. Dr Schmitz [the Rector of the High School of Edinburgh, a German] gives him lectures on Roman history. Italian, German, and French are advanced at the same time; and three times a week the Prince drills with the 16th Hussars, who are stationed in the city.

Mr Fisher, who is to be his tutor at Oxford, was also in Holyrood. Law and history are the subjects in which he is to prepare the Prince. . . .

The eldest son was still misunderstood.

In October, as usual, the Queen returned reluctantly to Windsor. Her passion for the Highlands was undimmed; and when her daughter ventured to express her affection for 'dear, dear Windsor', its châtelaine sent a fairly sharp retort.

> I must say that (though I know the feeling for 'home' prompts you to say it) the appellation of 'dear, dear Windsor', coming at this moment, when I am struggling with my homesickness for my beloved Highlands, the air – the life, the liberty – cut off for so long – almost could make me angry. . . .
>
> I miss these people [at Balmoral] so much. It is soothing and refreshing when one is in such an isolated position as we are, to be able to talk freely with those below you, and to find such open independence, such sense and such affection for you.

The confession may explain much about the Queen's affection, in later years, for her personal servant, John Brown.

Meanwhile, at Windsor, the Queen who read novels by Kingsley and Charlotte M. Yonge, and found 'not enough romance' in *Barchester Towers*, and revelled in *Jane Eyre*, turned back again to *Adam Bede*. 'Dear papa', she told her daughter, 'was much amused and interested by *Adam Bede*, which I am delighted to read a second time. There is such knowledge of human nature, such truth in the characters. I like to trace a likeness to the dear Highlanders in Adam – and also in Lisbeth and Mrs Poyser.'

The new year, 1860, was happily danced in. On 10 February, his twentieth wedding anniversary, the Prince wrote to Stockmar: 'We cannot be sufficiently grateful for many a blessing and many a success!' The Queen sent a postscript: 'One little word on this blessed day! Words cannot express my gratitude and my happiness. I wish I could think I *had made* one as happy as he has made me.'

As for politics, the Queen felt far from happy about them. Napoleon III was about to annex Nice and Savoy, as a reward for the military aid which he had given Victor-Emmanuel. On 7 March the Queen lamented to Princess Frederick William: 'We have been a good deal plagued lately with tiresome and annoying business, which unfortunately dear Papa will take too much to heart, and then it makes him unwell always – and affects his sleep. He really ought not to do so, because it makes ones life so difficult if one minds things so much as to make oneself ill.'

Next day they went to Osborne, and he forgot his annoyances in looking at his plants and listening to the birds. The Queen immersed herself in Tennyson's *Idylls of the King* ('so very peculiar, quaint and poetic'). The Prince, too, was absorbed in them, and asked the Poet Laureate to inscribe his copy. 'You would thus add a peculiar interest to the book containing those beautiful songs. . . . They quite rekindle the feeling with which the legends of King Arthur must have inspired the chivalry of old.'

Arthurian legend offered a welcome escape from the pressures of the modern world. Writing to his eldest daughter on 23 May, the Prince complained that he was 'tortured' by the prospect of two public dinners,

> at which I am, or rather shall be, in the chair. The one gives me seven, the other ten toasts and speeches, appropriate to the occasion, and distracting to myself. Then I have to resign at Oxford the Presidency of the British Association, and later in the season to open the Statistical Congress of all nations. Between these come the laying the foundation stone of the Dramatic College, the prize-giving at Wellington College, &c., &c.; and this, with the meetings of my different Commissions, and the delectable Ascot races. . . .

With Ascot came the first intimation that Princess Alice might soon marry. Among the guests at Windsor for Ascot week was Prince Louis of Hesse, who was clearly drawn to her. In July Princess Frederick William reported that the Hesse family were making overtures for a marriage.

August brought Balmoral. 'The house is unusually cold, but

open windows and fires will I hope set all right', the Queen reported briskly to her daughter. 'The heather is not yet out, but the bell heather and french heather of which I send you 2 little bits are most beautiful, in brilliant patches, as well as every sort of wild flower you can imagine!' The Queen's vitality had never been more evident. 'We had a very gay Ball last night', she announced on 8 September, 'and I, old woman [of forty-one], danced a great deal and I do so enjoy reels'.

On 22 September, the Queen and the Prince sailed from Gravesend for Antwerp on their way to Coburg. Princess Frederick William and her husband were to meet them there with the grandson whom they had not yet seen. They saw their grandchild daily at Coburg ('such a very charming, engaging little thing. God bless him!'). They saw Ernest and Alexandrina, they saw the ageing Stockmar, and they visited Florschütz, the Prince's old tutor, in the house which his two pupils had built for him. Stockmar was shocked by the Prince's melancholy. 'God have mercy on us, if something really serious happened to the Prince! It would kill him!' On the last morning of the visit, Albert asked his brother to walk to the fortress with him. The formidable old stronghold, on the top of its hill, looked majestically down on the town of Coburg. Suddenly Albert stopped, and Ernest saw the tears on his face. Albert had never ceased to belong to Coburg, and he knew that he was seeing it for the last time.

In November, after a highly successful visit to Canada, the Prince of Wales returned to Windsor. 'He is grown and has become so much more manly,' reported Lady Augusta Bruce, 'while he retains that sort of youthful simplicity and freshness which give his manner such charm.'

Late in November Prince Louis of Hesse came back to Windsor, to win Princess Alice. The betrothal occurred within the week. Princess Alice was only seventeen, and her future husband was twenty-three. Their engagement strengthened the family ties between England and Germany. Both the Queen and the Prince considered it highly satisfactory ('we like darling Louis . . . daily more', the Queen reported early in December. 'He is quite one of the family already').

The Queen had long been concerned with arranging a far more

Princess Alexandra of Denmark, (1862. Reproduced by gracious permission of Her Majesty The Queen.

momentous marriage. She had been looking for a wife for the Prince of Wales. 'What are we to do?' asked Princess Frederick William. 'Unfortunately, princesses do not spring up, like mushrooms out of the earth. . . . I sit continually with the Gotha Almanack in my hands turning the leaves over in hopes to discover someone who has not come to light!' The *Almanach de Gotha* was perused and re-perused, reputations and rumours were weighed. A few days after Princess Alice had been 'safely brought into port', the Queen thanked her eldest daughter for some photographs, and decided: 'The one of Princess Alexandra is indeed lovely!'

The year 1861 began with every prospect of domestic happiness. The death of the King of Prussia, who had been insane since 1857, could only be considered a deliverance, and on the accession of his brother, Prince William, who had been acting as Regent, Prince Frederick William became Crown Prince ('I flatter myself', the Queen had written, mildly, 'that Fritz will not complain of me as a mother-in-law?'). There were happy anniversaries to follow, and first came the third anniversary of Vicky's wedding. Then came the twenty-first anniversary of the Queen's own marriage. 'Very few', she told King Leopold, 'can say with me that their husband, at the end of twenty-one years, is not only full of the friendship, kindness and affection which a truly happy marriage brings with it, but of the same tender love as in the very first days.' 'You must promise', she reminded her daughter, 'to be with us for our silver wedding D.V. which will be in four years – if God spares us – as I trust He will.' The Prince gave his wife a present 'which he got at Coburg – from Gotha – a large elastic bracelet like a cuff – and so pretty'. 'We have faithfully kept our pledge for better or for worse', he told his mother-in-law, the Duchess of Kent, 'and [we] have only to thank God, that He has vouchsafed so much happiness to us.'

The Duchess of Kent was now seventy-five, and in the past two years she had suffered several attacks of erysipelas. Her right arm was so swollen and painful that on 9 March an operation had to be performed. Then her left arm and side were seen to be affected. Her condition worsened steadily. On 16 March the

The Duchess of Kent, who died on 16 March 1861, aged seventy-five. Daguerreotype by Antoine Claudet, July 1856. Reproduced by gracious permission of Her Majesty The Queen.

Queen – who had never witnessed death – was with her when she died.

Victoria had owed her childhood unhappiness largely to her mother; it had taken the Prince's patient diplomacy to bring them together after her marriage. But her mother's death now shocked her profoundly. This was the first great sorrow of her life. 'How touching She is in Her grief,' wrote Lady Augusta, '– how loving, – how humble – how full of faith and unquestioning trust. And the Prince – could you have seen his tears – could you see his sorrow now – His gentle thought and consideration – His fondness for the Queen – Oh! may God bless them in their Children and reward them.'

Queen Victoria was, in most things, eminently sensible; but to her the indulgence of grief was the actual measure of love. 'You must promise me', she had written to her daughter, recently, 'that if I should die your child or children and those around you should mourn; this really must be, for I have such strong feeling on the subject.' She herself was determined to mourn the death of her mother to the full; and she indulged her sorrow now.

> Your very kind and feeling letter touched me *deeply* [this to Lady Canning]. Such *universal sympathy* in my *overwhelming* grief, *such* love & respect for the memory of that *dearly* beloved mother were seldom seen, & I *have* felt it *gratefully – deeply*. But oh! dear Lady Canning, to lose a *Mother* & *such* a Mother, from whom except for a very few months I had *never* been parted, whom I heard from & wrote to, almost daily – *whose* love for me & mine *exceeded* everything. . . . is *dreadful! What* I have gone thro' & suffered in spite of the love & affection of *all* those *so dear* & near me – only *those* who *have* lost a *loving* Mother *can* tell!

The funeral took place on 25 March, at St George's Chapel, Windsor. Princess Frederick William came, briefly, from Berlin to comfort her mother. Alas, the Queen refused to be comforted. Early in April she confessed to her daughter: 'You are right, my dear child, I do not wish to feel better. . . . The relief of tears is great – and though since last Wednesday night I have had no very violent outburst – they come again and again every day, and are soothing to the bruised heart and soul.' A few days later, from Osborne:

> Don't worry yourself about me. I love to dwell on her, and to be

A picnic in the Highlands, 16 October 1861. The last Scottish expedition with the Prince Consort. L. to R.: Princess Alice, her fiancé Prince Louis of Hesse, Princess Helena, the Prince Consort, Queen Victoria. Engraving by J. A. S. Stephenson after the watercolour by Carl Haag. Reproduced by gracious permission of Her Majesty The Queen.

quiet and not to be roused out of my grief! To wish me to shake it off – and to be merry – would be to wish me no good! I could not and would not! Daily do I feel more the blank – the loss I *shall* experience – and the power of enjoying other things is not possible at present. Don't expect it or wish it, dear, for it cannot be! Young people with their elastic spirits are different and can hardly understand – the sort of quiet, serious state of mind which I am in and wish to remain in.

Court mourning for the Duchess of Kent had given the Queen and her husband respite from public affairs. They paid a prolonged visit to Osborne. 'On our leaving Osborne (which cost me much) on our voyage – our journey – how I missed and miss her!' So the Queen lamented. In Dublin, where she and the Prince found themselves late in August, Victoria reflected, at

last, on the nature of love. Perhaps there had been something lacking in Albert's devotion? 'I know that no one, not even dearest Papa, ever loved me as [Grandmama] did! Besides maternal love is a so different love – even if the other may be as great! And then woman's love exceeds what man's, I think, can ever be? That tenderness, that intense devotion, that attention – and delicate attention – in all trifles as beloved Grandmama possessed and showed – no man can have – and I feel that loss of all this – as life goes on – as each season passes – most acutely.'

At Balmoral, with the Prince's help, the Queen began to recover from her paroxysms of grief. Her children were about her. Princess Beatrice, entrancing as ever, had learned the story of Moses being found in the bulrushes, and obtained her mother's permission to bring him home if she found him in the Dee. Lady Augusta Bruce, reporting the agreement, added that Princess Beatrice 'mixes up Moses and Herod and all, and pretends to read. "And the Naughty Men killed the children and the Mothers cried *wipperly*."'

The Queen remained all too ready to weep. Even when she and her husband were together, she sometimes found it easier to talk to him on paper. Before they left Balmoral, she sent him a memorandum, grieving over the prospect of the return to Windsor.

> I can give you a very good certificate this time [the Prince replied] and am pleased to witness with you your own improvement. . . .
>
> My advice to be less occupied with yourself and your own feelings is really the kindest I can give, for pain is felt chiefly by dwelling on it and can thereby be heightened to an *unbearable extent*. . . . If you will take increased interest in things unconnected with personal feelings, you will find the task much lightened of governing those feelings in general which you state to be your great difficulty in life. God's assistance and support will not fail you in your endeavour.

It was cool and wise advice, dictated by deep affection; it suggests the patience and self-control which the Prince had sometimes needed to exercise.

By the end of October the Court was back at Windsor. On 9 November they even allowed themselves some gaiety, when the Prince of Wales came over from Cambridge to celebrate his

Prince Leopold with Lady and Miss Bowater at Cannes, February 1862 Reproduced by gracious permission of Her Majesty The Queen.

twentieth birthday. 'The band played for the first time since our sad loss.'

Another cloud was now hanging over the Queen and her husband. Their youngest son, who was eight years old, was exceedingly delicate. 'P. Leopold', Lady Augusta had written during the summer, 'is so delicate that Dr Jenner will not think him safe till the measles are quite over. His veins are too weak and he is subject for the least thing to bleeding, sometimes from the nose, sometimes internal. It is doubtful whether he may grow up, but they fear never to be a strong man.' Prince Leopold had been found to suffer from haemophilia, and the doctors had decided that he should spend the winter in the south of France. He had left Windsor on 2 November. 'He cried when I kissed him – and wished him good-bye', the Queen told her daughter, '– but he was in good spirits otherwise'. On 6 November she added: 'The good news of these last 2 days have cheered us much and relieved our anxiety. Really I think if they had not been better I should have sent off Dr Jenner or have started ourselves. I

began to get very fidgety at no improvement – and so many leeches alarmed us all.'

There was a further cause for anxiety. The Prince Consort had arranged the journey, and he had chosen the little boy's travelling companion. This was General Sir Edward Bowater, Groom in Waiting to the Queen, and a veteran of Waterloo. He was seventy-four. The choice was surprising, and it was disastrous. Soon after the General arrived in Cannes, he himself fell ill. 'Poor Sir Edward is sinking!' the Queen told her daughter. 'It is very sad. Mr Cavendish will go out shortly to be in readiness to do whatever is needed.' Before the end of the year, Sir Edward died.

On 12 November came the news that King Pedro of Portugal had succumbed to typhoid. He was only twenty-five, and a favourite cousin of the Queen and her husband. 'My Albert loved him like a son', Victoria wrote in her journal; and, in a letter to Princess Frederick William, she confessed: 'I have been much shaken again – but try to bear up as dear Papa (who has many worries) is so dejected.'

On the evening after he learned of King Pedro's death, the Prince heard some news which, according to the Queen, 'broke my Angel's heart'. During the summer, camping with the army at the Curragh, in Kildare, the Prince of Wales had been involved with an actress.

Such an escapade might seem natural for a young man of twenty, especially for one whose childhood and youth had been so rigorously supervised. The Prince Consort took a different view. The profligate behaviour of his father and his brother had given him a horror of promiscuity. The lofty counsels of his tutor, Florschütz, had confirmed his disgust. He himself had never been tempted by women. Casual relationships 'depressed him, grieved him, horrified him'. When the Prince of Wales was born, he had said 'the greatest object must be to make him as unlike as possible to any of his [Hanoverian] great-uncles'. When the Prince of Wales was two, Stockmar had written: 'Your Royal Highness can never rate too highly the importance of the life of the Prince of Wales, or of his good education; for . . . every shortcoming in his training and culture is certain to be avenged upon his father.' Now the Prince felt that his son's self-indulgence might damage the ideals for which he and the Queen had worked since their marriage.

On 20 November he wrote to the Prince of Wales, assuring him that those around him would do everything to help him, 'but they will be powerless unless they be met on your part with that openness and honesty which must characterize the dealings of gentlemen towards each other'. On 22 November he went to Sandhurst to inspect the new Staff College and Royal Military Academy; but he remained obsessed by his son's behaviour. He was all the more obsessed as he was far from well. Three days later he went to Cambridge to see the Prince of Wales. They had an outspoken conversation, and they were reconciled; but the Prince Consort remained in deep depression. In the evening he had a fit of shivering, and he was obliged to stay the night at Madingley.

The Prince was a large man, but he was not robust. In the last few years his health had gradually declined, his gastric attacks had grown more frequent, and his fits of sleeplessness more confirmed. From the middle of November, he virtually ceased to sleep, and on his return from Cambridge on 26 November he complained of pains in his back and legs, weakness and exhaustion. Next day the Queen told her daughter:

> Dearest Papa has written to you that he is not well – and so he is – but thank God! *unberufen* not one of his bad, old attacks – but a cold with neuralgia – a great depression which has been worse these last 3 days – but I hope will be much better tomorrow. The sad part is – that this loss of rest at night (worse than he has ever had before) was caused by a great sorrow and worry, which upset us both greatly – but him, especially – and it broke him quite down. I never saw him so low.

Two days later the Prince watched the Queen reviewing the Eton Volunteers. The weather was mild, but he wore a fur-lined coat. On Sunday, 1 December, he got up, as usual, at seven o'clock, and modified a despatch which the Foreign Office proposed to send to the American Government.

Since the spring of 1861, the Civil War had been raging in America. On 8 November, a Federal warship had stopped the British mail steamer *Trent* and arrested two Confederate agents who were on board. The British Cabinet resolved to demand satisfaction for the insult to the British Flag and for the breach of international law. The garrison in Canada was reinforced, and the British Press adopted a threatening tone. Lord John Russell –

recently created Earl Russell – submitted to the Queen the draft of a strong, uncompromising Note which he intended to send to Lord Lyons, the British envoy in Washington. 'The Queen', replied the Prince Consort, 'returns these important Drafts, which upon the whole she approves; but she cannot help feeling that the main Draft – that for communication to the American Government – is somewhat meagre. She should have liked to see the expression of a hope, that the American captain did not act under instructions, or, if he did, that he mis-apprehended them. . . .'

On the Prince's advice, the official Note was modified. His final sentence gave the American Government a means of saving face, and of releasing the Confederates, and it relieved the critical tension between England and America. 'There can be no doubt', Lord Palmerston was to tell the Queen, 'that, as Your Majesty observes, the alterations made in the Despatch to Lord Lyons contributed essentially to the satisfactory settlement of the dispute. But these alterations were only one of innumerable instances of the tact and judgment, and the power of nice discrimination which excited Lord Palmerston's constant and unbounded admiration.'

It was the last draft that the Prince Consort wrote: his last political act. As he handed the paper to the Queen, he said: 'I could scarcely hold my pen.' He attempted to write to Prince Leopold, but he gave up after the first few sentences. He went to matins that morning, and attended a luncheon party, but he ate nothing. On the following morning he did not dress, and the Court physicians were summoned to attend him.

Private nurses were then unknown, and – strange and irresponsible as it must seem – the Prince was tended by his personal servants, his private secretaries, and Princess Alice. On 4 December the Queen reported: 'Beloved Papa is improving, and I hope now each day will make a decided difference. But he is so depressed and so low – that it is always very distressing and the amount of sleepless nights has lowered him, besides the impossibility to touch food is very vexatious. . . . He likes being read to constantly. I have had to put our visitors for tomorrow off.'

The Prince's doctors seem to have decided that he must be indulged in his fever. They let him wander through his rooms at will.

I have lived through 3 days of dreadful anxiety [wrote the Queen on 6 December] – though there was not one alarming or unfavourable sympton. I feel so shaken – as for four nights I had not more than two or three hours' sleep! And though I slept more last night and for Papa's sake slept in the next room – I was for two hours in such a state of anxious suspense listening to every sound – that I feel very trembly myself. . . . Beloved Papa has never been confined to his bed, and is dressed and walks about his rooms. He is very irritable today. Dr Jenner has been most attentive, and is excellent, very clever, very kind and very determined.

Good Alice is a very great comfort – she is so devoted to dear Papa and reads to him and does every thing she can to help and cheer me! There is nothing now, my darling child, to be alarmed about – but I own that the trials this year – have made me feel very old!

Next day, 7 December, the doctors admitted that the Prince was suffering from gastric or low fever – the old fashioned euphemism for typhoid. That day, as he lay in bed, he told his wife that he heard birds singing, which made him think of his childhood at the Rosenau. Sometimes he rambled, and then again he would stroke her cheek, or lean his face on her shoulder. Once he asked for music, and Princess Alice played 'Ein feste Burg ist unser Gott' on the piano.

The Prince had never clung to life. 'I am sure', he had said, not long ago, 'that if I had a severe illness, I should give up at once, and should not fight for my life. I am not tenacious of it.' He had spoken without a trace of sadness. Now he made no resistance to illness. From the first, he was convinced that he was dying.

There is no evidence that the Queen blamed the doctors for his death. She believed, with all the tenacity of her nature, that her husband died from worry over the Prince of Wales; and that belief was fortified in the early days of the illness when the doctors assured her that the Prince Consort was simply ill from worry and overwork. In his review of the case, Sir James Clark recorded: 'There was excessive mental excitement on one very recent occasion.' This explains why the Prince called for the Prince of Wales's governor, General Bruce, when he was delirious. This explains why the Queen refused to summon the Prince of Wales to his father's deathbed. It also explains her antipathy for the Prince of Wales in his young manhood: an antipathy which she did not try to hide.

On 12 December the relations and Cabinet Ministers were informed of the Prince's critical condition. His Private Secretary told Lord Palmerston. The Prime Minister had been kept informed of every phase of the Prince's illness, and today he sent three letters to the Private Secretary. In the last, he wrote in terms so horrified that one wonders how the Prince and Palmerston had warred so constantly and for so long.

> My dear Phipps,
>
> Your telegram and letter have come upon me like a thunderbolt. I know that the disorder is one liable to sudden and unfavourable turns, but I had hoped that it was going on without cause for special apprehension. The result which your accounts compel me to look forward to as at least possible, is in all its bearings too awful to contemplate. One can only hope that Providence may yet spare us so dreadful a calamity.

On 13 December, Sir James Clark decided that the Queen must be warned of the danger. Lady Augusta took the courage to go to her room. 'It was a terrible moment, a life of anguish and agony was concentrated in it. . . . It was terrible to witness, but especially terrible to know what to say. The idea of what might be, she could scarcely bear. . . .' Constantly the Queen repeated: 'The country! Oh, the country! I could perhaps bear my own misery, but the poor country!'

Princess Frederick William was in Berlin; Prince Alfred was at sea, and Prince Leopold was still in Cannes. The Prince of Wales was in Cambridge. The Queen refused to send for him. Sir Charles Phipps telegraphed to summon him. He came by special train, and arrived at three o'clock on the morning of 14 December. Sir Henry Holland saw him on his arrival, and told him of his father's condition. 'The Prince of Wales' appearance they thought might alarm him', Lady Augusta was to remember, 'but it did not'. When the Queen returned to her husband's bedroom, at about ten o'clock, she found the Prince of Wales beside his bed.

The day continued; and, as evening fell, the doctors grew increasingly despondent.

> About six the Queen sent for Sir Charles [Phipps], and a terrible burst of misery ensued. After this [recalled Lady Augusta] she returned again to the sick room, calm and almost cheerful, and the beloved invalid was able to notice her, and return her expressions and

gestures of affection. . . . The children had been in the room one after the other; he smiled to them but did not speak. . . . The lamp was sinking. Towards 9.30 the Queen had another burst of misery and asked for the Dean [of Windsor], who spoke beautifully, and she no less: so humble, so meek, so loving, so strong in the feeling of duty.

Princess Alice, Prince and Princess Leiningen, Prince of Wales and Princess Helena were in the room. . . . Poor Princess Helena could not bear it. The doctors did not like her to be near her father, poor lamb; I did not know what to do with her. Princess Alice was in the sick room. She whispered to me with great calm, 'that is the death rattle', and went for her mother.

Then in the darkened room they knelt: the Queen and her elder children, . . . watching in agonized silence, the passing of that lofty and noble soul.

At quarter to eleven that night, the Prince Consort died.

Oh, how dreadful it was! The Queen fell upon him, called him by every endearing name; then sank into our arms, and let us lead or

carry her away to the adjoining room, when she lay on the sofa; then she summoned the children around her, to clasp them to her heart and assure them she would endeavour, if she lived, to live for them and her duty, and to appeal to them from henceforth to walk in the footsteps of him whom God had taken to Himself.

To Princess Frederick William she wrote: 'My darling Angel's child, Our Firstborn, God's will be done'.

The room in which the Prince Consort died, Windsor Castle, 14 December 1861. There are two beds because the Prince was frequently changed from one to the other to make him more comfortable. The further bed is probably the one in which he died. Reproduced by gracious permission of Her Majesty The Queen.

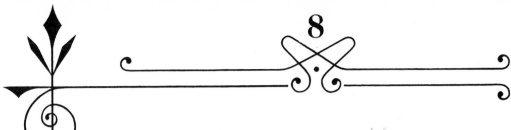

Victoria and Albert

The Prince, at forty-two, in the prime of manhood, had succumbed to a brief attack of fever. The public understandably felt that his illness had been mishandled. The team of doctors was unlikely to inspire confidence. Sir James Clark, aged seventy-three, was remembered for his mistaken diagnosis in the case of Lady Flora Hastings. He had been assisted by another septuagenarian, Sir Henry Holland, who had made his name as the medical attendant on Caroline of Brunswick, the demented wife of the Prince Regent. Lord Clarendon decided that these eminent practitioners 'had not been fit to attend a sick cat'.

It is true that the doctors had been ridiculously optimistic. 'Good, kind old Sir James', as the Queen described him, had constantly assured her that 'there is no cause for alarm, either present or future'. But one must not condemn these doctors by contrasting their treatment with modern practice. They no doubt did their utmost; and Sir James wrote, years later: 'On looking back I have the satisfaction, after viewing the case in all its bearings, of feeling that everything was done to save him that human art, as far as is present known, could do.'

The Prince Consort had died of typhoid fever. The drains of Windsor, condemned years ago and never put in order, had done their work. But he himself had not wanted to live. 'I do not cling to life', he had told the Queen. 'You do; but I set no store by it. If only I was assured that those I love were well cared for, I should be quite ready to die tomorrow'. Neither his sense of duty, nor his love for his wife and children, had compelled him to fight. 'He *would* die', the Queen said, later, to Lord Derby. 'He seemed not to care to live. He died from want of what they call pluck.'

She adored him, but she acknowledged his weakness and, perhaps, his final selfishness.

On 18 December, with Princess Alice, the Queen went to Frogmore, and chose the site for the Royal Mausoleum. On 19 December she moved to Osborne. She was to stay there until after the funeral.

The Prince Consort was dressed, for burial, in the uniform of a Field-Marshal: the uniform which he had worn at his wedding. A wreath of flowers made by Princess Alice was laid on his breast. A miniature of his wife was set in his hands.

His funeral took place in St George's Chapel, Windsor, on Monday, 23 December, and, in accordance with his wishes, it was as simple as tradition allowed. The Prince of Wales and Prince Arthur were chief mourners. When the coffin was lowered into the vault, and the handfuls of earth were scattered on it, the Prince of Wales burst into tears. Before the vault was closed, a Queen's Messenger from Osborne brought three little wreaths and a bouquet. The wreaths, of moss and violets, had been made by the three elder Princesses. The bouquet of violets, with a white camellia in the centre, had been sent by the Queen. These homely tributes were laid on the pall which covered the coffin; and, as a contemporary observed, they were 'mementoes of domestic love and worth above all the heraldry that ever was emblazoned'.

The nation went into mourning; and a flood of tracts and sermons swept the country. At Crathie, near Balmoral, Dr Macleod delivered an address which must have touched Queen Victoria's heart. Few men who ever lived, he said,

> no Prince certainly of whom we read, could have possessed a mind so many-sided with such corresponding political and social influence. He was indeed the type of a new era, an era of power; but not of that kind of power represented by the armour of his noble ancestors, the power of mere physical strength, courage, or endurance, displayed at the head of armies, or of fleets; but the moral power of character, the power of intellectual culture, of extensive knowledge, of earnest thought; the power of the sagacious statesman, of the *single-minded good man*: that power which discerns, interprets, and guides the wants and the spirit of the age.

At Eversley Church, on the eve of the Prince's funeral, a sermon was preached by the Reverend Charles Kingsley, chaplain-in-ordinary to the Queen, and Professor of Modern History at Cambridge. For many years, said Kingsley, the Prince

> has committed his way unto the Lord; and the Lord has brought it to pass, and given him his heart's desire. He has seen grow up around him a virtuous court, a happy family, a country improving in civilization, education, peace, prosperity, content, freedom, loyalty, such as Britain never saw before; he has seen all that he worked at (and he worked long and heavily at a hundred matters of which the world knew little or naught) prosper and succeed, because all his work was founded upon truth, and justice, and the fear of God. And if he needed one thing more, that thing, too, God has given him this day. He has at last made his righteousness as clear as the light. . . .
>
> And perhaps this was needed.
>
> For the truth is – and I think all true Britons feel it this day – that we were not altogether fair to the Prince. We dealt him hard measure at first. We felt for him too little faith, hope or charity. . . .
>
> It does not come altogether too late, – this praise of him, which rises from all true British hearts. Nothing upon earth, perhaps, could lighten the load of grief which lies upon the heart of our beloved Queen more, than to see her subjects honouring and loving him as he deserved.

Lord Palmerston was received in audience by the Queen at Osborne. He wept bitterly.

The news of the Prince's death had reached Coburg on 16 December. Stockmar, in his grief, wrote to Ernest II. 'In his search for comfort', the Duke remembered, 'he spoke of the marvellous perfection in which my brother's life passed harmoniously in a shorter span than is the usual destiny of mortals. He had attained a greatness which would assure him his place in history far more speedily than usually happens. Thus he had shaken off the weariness of an existence, which, being cut short at the moment of greatest success, would impress coming generations as a noble work of art.'

Disraeli wrote of the Prince Consort that 'he formed and guided his generation with benignant power'. This was true, for in its most marked characteristics the age was Albertian rather than Victorian. As Mr Fulford has emphasized, 'the years from 1840 to 1860 reveal a heightened interest in art, in music, an

increased awareness of social problems, a more general understanding of the charms of domestic felicity, and a vague striving
after higher things. One cannot argue that the Prince Consort
was solely responsible for these developments, but he undoubtedly gave them an impetus. He strove to set before the people
something worthier of worship than their own commercial and
material triumphs.' Whatever the demerits of nineteenth-
century England, its nobleness of purpose is still plain. Nobility
of character was the quality which the Prince most admired, and
by which he sought to guide his own existence.

He had not tired of benevolence. 'It was not the fancy of a day
with him. It was the sustained purpose of a life.' So wrote the
editor of his published speeches; and the same anonymous writer
continued that, if the Prince had lived, 'he would inevitably have
become the most accomplished statesman and the most guiding
personage in Europe – a man to whose arbitrement fierce national quarrels might have been submitted, and by whose influence
calamitous wars might have been averted.'

His supreme achievement at home was his contribution to the
theory and practice of constitutional monarchy. He had checked
the personal approach of Hanoverian politics; but he had established the essential and permanent influence of the Crown. He
had created the modern English monarchical tradition. And, as a
London journalist wrote, 'this man, who never sat upon our
Throne, and who ceased at the early age of forty-two to stand
beside it, did more than any of our Sovereigns – except very,
very few – to brighten its lustre and strengthen its foundations.
. . . His was a pure and lofty life, from which every man, and,
most of all, every Christian, may learn many an ennobling
lesson'. He had indeed been Albert the Good. 'Never in my life',
wrote his brother, 'have I met anyone who had so pure a
sympathy for humanity in the abstract. All that is beautiful and
noble which is expressed by the term "a philanthropic soul" was
always at work in him.'

There are certain striking parallels between Princess Charlotte
and Queen Victoria. Both of them were born of unlikely and
decidedly unpromising marriages. Both of them endured unhappy childhoods, torn between rival factions and warring

Princess Charlotte and Prince
Leopold at the Opera. Drawing by
George Dawe. Reproduced by
gracious permission of Her Majesty
The Queen.

relations. Each of them married a Prince of Saxe-Coburg, and each of them was transformed by the alliance. 'It is quite certain', wrote Charlotte, 'that [Leopold] is the only being in the world who would have suited me and who could have made me happy and a good woman. It is his celestial character, his patience, his kindness, and nothing else would have succeeded. . . . In fact, he has all my confidence, he is master of all my thoughts, of everything that I do. . . . The words might well have been written by Victoria about Albert; and, indeed, they virtually were. 'The Queen', she admitted, after his death, 'did nothing, thought of nothing, without her beloved and gracious husband, who was her support, her constant companion, her guide, who helped her in *everything*, great and small.'

The Saxe-Coburgs had a driving sense of purpose, unrelenting industry, and remarkable political acumen. They had (however Leopold behaved in later years) a rigid standard of morality, a deep belief in the domestic virtues. They gave their wives a sense of security. They were masterful, and their wives were grateful for their absolute domination. The Saxe-Coburgs were also quite without endearing qualities. They were exceptionally handsome – but they had no charm, no humour, and little human warmth – or human weakness. They were pedantic and curiously cold. Charlotte and Victoria were warm, impulsive, generous and spirited, they had a sharp sense of humour and abundant Hanoverian vitality. Posterity must sometimes feel surprised by their hero-worship of their husbands. Yet worship them they did; and the Coburg marriages remain among the high romances of nineteenth-century English history.

Both ended prematurely, but though the death of Charlotte is perennially touching, the death of Albert somehow fails to move us. Despite our admiration, we cannot care about him. Perhaps he seems too perfect; perhaps he is too resolutely foreign. The true Coburger had never felt deep affection for his adopted country: Perhaps that is why it has never felt affection for him.

'Even the poor people in small villages, who don't know me, are shedding tears for me, as if it were their own private sorrow.' So Victoria wrote, when Albert died. Like her contemporaries, we still grieve for her rather than with her. It is true that Albert of Saxe-Coburg had been the perfect husband for Victoria. It is true that for the rest of her life – another forty years – she rarely ceased to mourn him. At forty-two, she was left a widow, isolated by bereavement as she was by the splendour of her status. No one could deny the personal tragedy. 'The whole house seems like Pompeii', wrote Lady Augusta Bruce, when the Prince had died, 'the life suddenly extinguished'.

And yet there remains – at least for us – a quiet, but persistent and undeniable sense of relief. When her husband died, Queen Victoria was free to be herself. In the first years of her reign, she had shown her brilliant, instinctive sense of sovereignty. She had known that she alone was born for the Crown. Victoria was a Queen by birth, and a Queen in every fibre of her being. But for twenty years her husband had dominated her life. Now once more she found herself alone. A new and glorious reign had begun.

Greatness had been born in her, and she had not changed her nature; marriage had only made her wiser and more mature. And from that marriage, as the Prince had prophesied to Stockmar, 'much good would yet be engendered for the world'. Queen Victoria's marriage had made the British monarchy secure: not only as a political institution, but as a lasting example of personal excellence. As one of her subjects wrote: 'She reigns for her virtues supreme in the affections of Englishmen. An Englishman is proud of his country, but above all of his Queen.'

It was left to an unknown journalist, in the *Boston Watchman and Recorder*, to pay Prince Albert's wife the final tribute:

> She has restored to loyalty its old prestige. She has once more surrounded it with the reverential affection which makes obedience so easy, patriotism so hearty, and constitutional government so strong and stable. She has revived and given a new lease of life to sentiments which have slumbered since the Stuart days, and which some had mourned over as altogether dead. She has done this by a combination of qualities which is rare in any rank; rarest, perhaps of all, upon a throne. But most of all has she effected it by setting an example in her household life of private and domestic virtue, which Britons appreciate so much, and by never in a single instance belying the confidence of the nation.

Queen Victoria, more than any other Sovereign in our past, commands our affection and our admiration. We are still, in a manner of speaking, her subjects today.

Select Bibliography

Queen Victoria, *Letters from a Journal of Our Life in the Highlands, 1848-1861*, Helps, A. (ed.) (Smith, Elder, & Co., 1868). *More Leaves from a Journal of our Life in the Highlands, 1862-1882* (Smith, Elder, & Co., 1884).

Benson, E. F., *Queen Victoria* (Longmans, 1935).

Benson, A. C. and Esher, Viscount (eds), *The Letters of Queen Victoria, 1837-1861*, 3 vols (Murray, 1907).

Bolitho, H. and Windsor, Dean of (eds), *Letters of Lady Augusta Stanley* (Gerald Howe, 1927).

Fulford, Roger, *The Prince Consort* (Macmillan, 1949).

Fulford, Roger (ed.), *Dearest Child*. Letters between Queen Victoria and the Princess Royal, 1858-1861 (Evans Bros, 1964).

Grey, The Hon., *The Early Years of the Prince Consort* (Smith, Elder, & Co., 1867).

Jagow, Dr Kurt (ed.) and Dugdale, E. T. D. (trans.), *Letters of the Prince Consort, 1831-1861* (Murray, 1938).

Esher, Viscount (ed.), *The Girlhood of Queen Victoria*. A selection from Her Majesty's diaries, 1832-1840 (Murray, 1912).

Longford, Elizabeth, *Victoria R. I.* (Weidenfeld & Nicolson, 1964).

Martin, Sir Theodore, *The Life of His Royal Highness the Prince Consort*, 5 vols (Smith, Elder, & Co., 1875-80).

Surtees, Virginia, *Charlotte Canning*. Lady-in-Waiting to Queen Victoria and wife of the first Viceroy of India, 1817-1861 (Murray, 1975).

Tytler, Sarah, *The Life of Her Most Gracious Majesty the Queen*, 3 vols (J. S. Virtue, 1897).

Woodham-Smith, Cecil, *Queen Victoria* (Hamish Hamilton, 1972).

Index